IMAGES OF WAR
JAPAN TRIUMPHANT

This Thompson sub-machine-gunner of the Manchester Regiment is on jungle exercises in Malaya in the months leading up to war with Japan. Any jungle training undertaken by the British and Australians in 1941 did not prepare them when encountering the superior field skills of the Japanese Imperial Army. Perhaps the foliage attached to his rather ungainly cork sun helmet as camouflage is symbolic of the difference between the two combatants. It sums up the lack of understanding on the part of the British command of what kind of enemy they were to face a few months later.

IMAGES OF WAR

JAPAN TRIUMPHANT

The Far East Campaign
1941–1942

RARE PHOTOGRAPHS FROM
WARTIME ARCHIVES

Philip Jowett

Pen & Sword
MILITARY

This book is dedicated to my inspiring mother, June, and to her much-loved father, Gunner John Smith-Pounder, who served in the 12th Battery, 6th Heavy Anti-Aircraft Regiment, Royal Artillery in Singapore in 1941. He, like most of his fellow artillerymen, was transferred to Java and fought as an infantryman during the fall of the Netherlands East Indies. Taken prisoner, he died in Pakan Baroe Japanese Prisoner of War Camp on Sumatra on 9 August 1945.

First published in Great Britain in 2019 by
PEN & SWORD MILITARY
an imprint of
Pen & Sword Books Ltd,
47 Church Street,
Barnsley, South Yorkshire, S70 2AS

Every effort has been made to trace the copyright of all the photographs.
If there are unintentional omissions, please contact the publisher in writing, who will correct all subsequent editions.

ISBN 978 1 52673 435 8

The right of Philip Jowett to be identified as Author of this Work has been asserted by him in accordance with the Copyright, Designs and Patents Act 1988.

A CIP record for this book is available from the British Library.

Typeset by CHIC GRAPHICS

Printed and bound by CPI Group (UK) Ltd, Croydon, CR0 4YY

Pen & Sword Books Ltd incorporates the imprints of Pen & Sword Aviation, Pen & Sword Family History, Pen & Sword Maritime, Pen & Sword Military, Pen & Sword Discovery, Wharncliffe Local History, Wharncliffe True Crime, Wharncliffe Transport, Pen and Sword Select, Pen and Sword Military Classics, Leo Cooper, The Praetorian Press, Remember When, Seaforth Publishing and Frontline Publishing and White Owl

For a complete list of Pen & Sword titles please contact
Pen & Sword Books Limited
47 Church Street, Barnsley, South Yorkshire, S70 2AS, England
E-mail: enquiries@pen-and-sword.co.uk
Website: www.pen-and-sword.co.uk

Contents

This poster for the Stadwacht, or City Guard, formed in 1940, says simply, 'The City Guard Watches'. The Stadwacht acted as a reserve force for the KNIL and had a similar role to that of the Home Guard in Britain. It was recruited from older retired soldiers of the KNIL as well as civilian volunteers, including foreign residents. Its volunteers wore a tin badge above their breast pocket which featured the region it was raised from.

Introduction

During a six-month period between early December 1941 and May 1942 the Japanese Imperial Army, Navy and Air Force conquered most of South-East Asia and much of the Pacific. This 'lightning' campaign was in reality a series of separate but inter-related campaigns which saw Japan gain huge territories. By May 1942 Japan had taken Malaya, Burma, Borneo, Hong Kong, the Philippines and the Netherlands East Indies. Japan also gained virtual control over French Indo-China and an alliance with the only independent South-East Asian country, Thailand. In addition, her conquests in the Pacific saw the occupation of any islands previously under British, US, Australian or Dutch rule. The carefully prepared campaign of conquest had been in the planning stages for many years and its success changed forever the political situation in the Far East. Although the peoples of South-East Asia were only effectively swapping one colonial master for another, they would not accept the return of their old masters post-1945.

After coming out of centuries of self-imposed isolation in the 1860s, Japan quickly showed that it had ambitions to create an empire for itself in Asia. From 1894 until 1941 the Japanese Imperial Army and Navy had concentrated on an aggressive 'Northern Road' doctrine which called for their domination of mainland China, Manchuria and Korea. This led to the Sino-Japanese War of 1894–5, the Russo-Japanese War of 1904–5, the Intervention in Siberia in 1919–22 and the invasions of Manchuria in 1931 and the rest of China in 1937. Other military theorists in Japan had called for a 'Southern Road' policy which would see the Japanese conquest of South-East Asia. This had the disadvantage of conflict with the Imperial Powers of Britain and the Dutch and in all probability the USA. From 1894 the Japanese had had a more or less free hand in mainland Asia defeating Imperial China, Imperial Russia and Nationalist China. Its invasion of Manchuria in 1931 and the rest of China in 1937 and the atrocities committed by the Imperial Army there led to widespread protests in the West. Whilst Europe was obsessed with the increasing threat of Nazi Germany, from 1933 the USA in particular focused on Japan's aggression against China. Japan walked out of the League of Nations in 1933 in protest at criticism of its war in China and expected the European powers and the USA to mind their own business. Its chief politicians and military leaders had already hatched plans to first defeat China and then 'move south'. This was the obvious conclusion of any switch from the Northern Road doctrine to the Southern Road doctrine. The term 'move south' described the plan to invade the colonial possessions of Great Britain and the Netherlands in South-East Asia. These included

British-ruled Burma, Malaya, Northern Borneo and the Royal Navy base on Singapore island on the southern tip of Malaya. The other main target for Japanese imperial expansion was the Netherlands East Indies which had vital oilfields that they coveted. Even though it was forecast that the oilfields in the Netherlands East Indies would run dry by 1944 they were still important to Japanese plans.

One thing that the Japanese wanted to avoid if at all possible was conflict with the USA as the US navy was seen as their potential main protagonist in the Pacific. The Japanese Imperial Navy may not have wanted a war with the USA but they had been planning for it anyway. If they did go to war the Philippines, which had been controlled by the USA since 1898, would then be added to the list of conquests. Growing public sympathy for Chinese people in the USA and in the more enlightened countries in Europe led eventually to the introduction of trade embargoes on Japan. To a country like Japan, which had little or no resources of its own apart from coal, its trade with the world was vital. Attempts to break these embargoes included, after 1940, putting pressure on the Dutch government in exile to allow 'peaceful' access to their oil supplies. The stubborn refusal by the Dutch government in exile in London to give into Japanese pressure added another 'nail in the coffin' of peace. After their mother country had been occupied by the Germans in May 1940, these exiled politicians were not in the mood to give into threats.

By October 1940 the Japanese had decided that the only way to gain the resources that its military machine badly needed was by conquest. In the USA the Roosevelt government imposed an 'Export Control Act' on 5 July 1940. This severely affected Japanese trade and heavily damaged Japan's industry as it could no longer import US goods. The USA's resolve to deal with Japan was further strengthened when the Japanese virtually took over French Indo-China in the summer of 1941. In July the USA froze all of Japan's assets in their country under Executive Order 8832 which effectively stopped the Japanese from buying oil in the world markets. Now it was only a matter of when not if the Japanese would strike as 1941 turned into a bad year for the empire. In addition to their other problems, by 1941 the stalemate in China had become a major manpower drain for the Japanese Imperial Army. With no sign of total victory, the number of troops killed since 1937 stood at 189,000. Although the Chinese had suffered many times the number of casualties, there was no sign of the expected capitulation by Chiang Kai-shek's Nationalist government. It now became more urgent for the Japanese to get badly needed resources from the colonial possessions of the British and Dutch in South-East Asia. If the Japanese were to maintain their campaign on the Chinese mainland then they would now have to open a second front and 'Strike South'.

Chapter One

Japan Prepares for War, 1940-1

Japan's plans for the conquest of South-East Asia depended largely on the 'co-operation' of the authorities in two places. These were the colonial administration in French Indo-China and the government of the independent Kingdom of Thailand. Both these territories would hopefully act as 'launching pads' for the Japanese Imperial Army's invasion of Malaya, Burma and the Philippines. After the defeat of France by Germany in June 1940 a collaborationist French government had been set up by the Germans in the spa town of Vichy to rule un-occupied parts of France. The Vichy French government was allowed by Germany to maintain control of its colonial possessions in Africa and South-East Asia. A pro-Vichy governor was installed in French Indo-China which was made up of modern day Vietnam, Cambodia and Laos. Japan now took advantage of the Vichy government's weakness to gain an important foothold in the region. The Japanese were interested in the northern Vietnamese ports which were strategically ideal as a jumping off point for any Japanese naval force aimed at South-East Asia. The new 'puppet' Vichy governor in Indo-China came under almost immediate pressure from Japan to allow its troops to garrison certain 'strategic' points in Indo-China. In addition, the Japanese asked for permission to use some of the French military airfields in the region. They also wanted to be able to unload their military supplies in the northern Vietnamese port of Hanoi. By September 1940 the stalling of the French governor led to an invasion of northern Vietnam and the local Vichy forces were soon defeated by the Japanese Imperial Army. The French had to back down and three airfields in Tonkin province were taken over by the Japanese air force whilst their troops were allowed to be stationed in several garrisons in Vietnam. This humiliation was followed in late 1940 by Japanese support for the Thai armed forces in a little-known war with the Vichy French. This border war, which was fought along the Thai–Cambodian border, was largely instigated by the Japanese. Even though the Thai army, navy and air force were outfought by the French, Japan's support for Thailand was to prove vital. In March 1941 the Japanese arbitrated a peace between the two warring factions and the agreement heavily favoured the Thai government. Japan had been involved in

Thailand for a number of years and had sent 500 military advisors to train its army in 1938. The Imperial Army now sought permission to use Thai territory and ports to invade Northern Malaya if necessary.

Although the Thai prime minister, General Phibun Songkhram, was pro-Japanese, he did not really want thousands of Imperial Army troops marching across Thai territory. Eventually he did agree to the Japanese use of the southern ports of Singora and Patani and the crossing of Thai territory to the Malayan border. He said he would allow this 'violation' of Thai territory in exchange for the return of some Thai provinces lost to Burma in the pre-colonial period. In addition, Thailand was to be offered several northern Malayan provinces after the defeat of the British. In the event the landings by Japanese troops at Singora in December 1941 were initially resisted by the local Thai forces. The Thai army was no match for the Japanese and a peace deal was soon agreed between the two parties. With Thailand now co-operating with the Japanese there was nothing to stop the Imperial Army using its territory to invade Malaya. A British air raid on the Thai capital Bangkok in January 1942 served to push Thailand further into the arms of the Japanese. In the same month the Thai prime minister signed an alliance with Japan pragmatically saying: 'time to declare war with the winner'.

Opposite above: Japanese troops cycle into the southern Indo-China city of Saigon in 1941, by which time they were in control of most strategic points throughout the region. They stationed troops and planes wherever they wanted and there was nothing that the Vichy officials could effectively do to stop them. The people of Vietnam, Cambodia and Laos were virtually swapping one colonial master for another. Indo-China could now be used as one of the jumping off points for Japan's conquest of South-East Asia.

Opposite below: Vichy French troops march out of one of their bases which has been occupied by the Japanese Imperial Army in 1941. During 1940 and 1941 a series of demands by the Japanese led to them taking over army and air force bases in Indo-China. Although most of these handovers were managed peacefully, any resistance by the French was met with brutality by the Imperial Army. In August 1945 when the Japanese occupied the whole of French Indo-China several thousand Vichy troops were massacred after resisting the takeover.

This photograph has been censored by the newspaper which published it by the whitewashing of the sign that this Japanese truck is passing. The image, however, shows the entry into French Indo-China of the Japanese Imperial Army in 1941. By July that year the Japanese had thrown away any pretence about their military presence in Vietnam. As their grip tightened over the region the Japanese also demanded that the Vichy authorities supply them with 80 per cent of the Indo-Chinese rice exports.

General Sumita visits French Vichy naval officers in Hanoi in northern Vietnam in the build-up to the war in 1941. As soon as the French were defeated by Germany in June 1940 their new collaborationist Vichy government came under pressure from the Japanese. Although Japan did not want to add French Indo-China to its empire officially, it did want to use its territory for its own war aims. The French would be allowed to govern Indo-China as long as they did as they were told by officers like Sumita.

As part of their agreement with the Vichy French government the Japanese were allowed to station their planes at several Indo-Chinese air bases. This Nakajima KI-27B fighter is being serviced and belongs to the 2nd Squadron, 84th Independent Fighter Company. The Japanese military presence in French Indo-China was a threat to Thailand and to Burma which both had borders with the territory.

Prince Konoye was the fairly moderate premier of Japan from July 1940 until mid-October 1941 when he and his supporters were ousted by General Tojo. He had been forced to resign because of his lack of support for the coming war with the USA and Britain by the warmongering Tojo. His pleas to Tojo to negotiate a withdrawal from China by the Japanese Army with the USA fell on deaf ears. Now that the moderate politicians were off the scene the slow Japanese drift towards war with the USA, which had begun in 1931, became a 'leap' under the aggressive Tojo and his clique of politicians and military officers.

The Japanese prime minister General Hideki Tojo had taken over from Prince Konoye as Japanese premier in October 1941. Tojo now held the portfolios of Home Minister and War Minister at the same time and was virtual dictator of Japan for much of the war. Tojo had supported Konoye in his earlier attempts to negotiate with the USA in his previous office of Army Minister. Tojo did have last-minute nerves about the dangerous course that Japan was taking and held off the decision to put the empire on a war footing for a few weeks after coming to power. By late November 1941 he was ready to commit the empire to all-out war with the USA, the Dutch and the British Empire.

Japanese bomber crews read their orders before taking off on a bombing raid over Thailand in 1941. The Japanese were determined to bring Thailand into their sphere of influence and needed to use the country's territory to invade Malaya and Burma. Luckily for Japan, the country's prime minister General Phibun Songkhram was pragmatically pro-Japanese. He realized that there was more to be gained than to be lost by making some kind of agreement with the Japanese. A British bombing raid on Bangkok in January 1942 gave Phibun the excuse he needed to forge an alliance with the Japanese Empire.

A Vickers heavy machine-gun crew of the Thai army practise anti-aircraft drill in the days before the Japanese invasion of their country. The Thai army had 44 infantry battalions, 9 cavalry battalions, 13 artillery groups, 6 engineer battalions and 3 armoured companies. In the border war with French Vichy forces in 1940 they had mobilized 50,000 men in 3 divisions. Although the army was reasonably well equipped with modern tanks, artillery and aircraft, it was no match for the seasoned Japanese Imperial Army.

General Phibun Songkhram (in the centre), the prime minister of Thailand in 1941, inspecting weaponry and equipment captured from the French Colonial Army in 1940–1. Thailand was supported by Japan in its conflict with Vichy France which was fought over former Thai regions in French Indo-China. With Japan's conditional backing the main objectives of the Thais were met and the Vichy French authorities had to cede territory. This Japanese support pulled General Phibun and his government further into their sphere of influence.

Chapter Two

The British Empire in the Far East Prepares, 1941

The British Empire covered the globe in the early decades of the twentieth century comprising colonies, protectorates and other possessions in the West Indies, Africa, Middle East and the Far East. Britain's imperial possessions in the Far East had grown in the late nineteenth century to include amongst others Malaya, Burma, Hong Kong and northern Borneo. During the First World War the British and its imperial forces had fought in Africa and the Middle East against the Germans and Ottoman Turks. Imperial Japan joined the Entente Powers and had fought against the Germans in China in 1914. Although seen by the West rather wistfully in military terms as 'jolly Oriental chaps', the Japanese soldiers had proven themselves as tough and often brutal fighters since 1894. The aggression of the Japanese in Manchuria and China made the rest of the world fully aware of their capabilities.

By the late 1930s it was obvious that the threat to the British Empire in the Far East now came from the Japanese. It was also recognized that measures would have to be taken to counter the threat of the Japanese but these were constrained by economic problems during the 1920s and 1930s. Like every other world nation, Great Britain had been badly affected by the Depression of the 1930s. The resulting shortage of funds led to a number of necessary defence economies which adversely affected the military forces in the Far East, and particularly during the 1930s. In Malaya for instance in the late 1930s the military budget was so tight that only £60,000 was allocated to improve the defences north of Singapore. Almost the whole of this paltry figure was spent on building machine-gun emplacements in the state of Johore in the south of Malaya. Likewise, British army units stationed in the Far East often saw their strength diminished by cuts, including in Burma. There the only British army units stationed in the late 1930s were the 1st Battalion of the Gloucestershire Regiment and a battalion of the 2nd King's Own Yorkshire Light Infantry. Both of these battalions had been further weakened by the stripping of some of their officers who had been transferred to India. This shortage of officers and NCOs meant that neither battalion could muster more than two companies' worth of troops.

As war with Japan grew more likely the various locally recruited volunteer units took on a new importance. Although they were seen as more important to their homeland's defence, their reliability was often called into question by the British officers in command of them. After the outbreak of war with Germany in September 1939 the imperial forces in the Far East were given even less priority. Reinforcements of men and equipment were not forthcoming and the Far East was at the back of the queue where both were concerned. When Britain was fighting for its survival in 1940 and 1941 the perceived threat from the Japanese was not as important as the very real and immediate threat from Nazi Germany. For this reason from September 1939 until December 1941 the British forces in the Far East received relatively little in the form of new military equipment. For the foreseeable future the British army in Burma, Malaya and the other Far Eastern possessions would have to make do largely with what they already had.

In September 1941 the total number of troops available to defend the British Empire in the East were, in Malaya, 11,000 British, 35,000 Indians, 25,000 Australians and about 17,000 Malayan volunteers. Burma was defended by 2,000 British, 7,000 Indian and 26,000 Burmese troops of doubtful value. Included in the Burmese total were the six battalions of the Burma Frontier Force (BFF) formed largely from units of the Burma Military Police. The personnel of the BFF were nearly all Indians or Gurkhas and there was no intention that they be used in the front line. Many of the local recruits for the Burmese units were suspected of disloyalty and of having sympathy with the Nationalist cause. Northern Borneo was divided into four separate 'protectorates' rather than colonies. These were the island of Labaun, Northern Borneo, Sarawak and Brunei, the first two having a British administration. Brunei was an independent sultanate which still depended for its protection on the British army, as did Sarawak. Sarawak was a kingdom which had been ruled since 1841 by a British family, one of whom held the hereditary position of rajah. The total force available to protect the whole of Northern Borneo was 1,000 Indian troops and 2,500 poorly trained volunteers. In December 1941 the Hong Kong garrison stood at 19,000, and 5,500 of this number were made up of local European and Asian volunteers. New Guinea, the huge island to the north of Australia, was divided down the middle between the Dutch and Australians. In 1941 the island was defended by a militia force recruited from the expatriate Australian population. This force was reinforced by three militia battalions which arrived in New Guinea between March and December 1941. The average age of the militia was 18 or 19 years old and these youths for several months in 1942 had to battle the invading Japanese army alone. There were also a number of New Guinea volunteer units formed with the first, the Papua Infantry Battalion, mustering about 600 men. In the Pacific the British-ruled islands usually had some kind of regular or paramilitary force to defend them. These were often small and poorly armed with Lee–Enfield rifles and the odd Bren gun, which was the heaviest weapon in use. The Kingdom of Tonga was ruled by Queen Salote Tupou III who gave her full support to the British. By early 1941 the Tongan Defence Force had 2,700 regulars and was backed by 10,000 part-time home guard soldiers.

These two photographs show the Burmese Frontier Force training with their mountain guns in September 1941. The BFF was made up largely of Indian units with some Burmese native units mixed in as well. In this photograph the gun crews are demonstrating their skills in unloading their guns from the mules carrying the dissembled parts. On the right of the photo the three gun crew hold the barrel of the gun using carrying poles ready to place it on the carriage on the left of the image.

In this second photograph the Indian artillerymen of the BFF are putting together their QF 3.7in howitzer Mk I gun. According to the original caption to the photograph it took a well-trained crew 1 minute to 'unlimber, assemble and get their mountain guns into action'. The original guns which were employed largely on the North-West Frontier had large shields but these were often removed in jungle conditions.

A machine-gun section of the Burma Rifles is given instruction in the operation of the Bren gun in the summer of 1941. The Burma Rifles recruited mainly from amongst the Burmese hill tribes such as the Karen, Kachin and Chin. When war became likely the original four battalions were doubled to eight but this was at the expense of their general performance. Some recruits for the expanded force had to come from the majority Burmese population who were regarded as 'unreliable'. By 1940 there were only about a 1,000 officers and men of Burmese extract in the Burma Rifles and BFF.

Soldiers of the 2nd King's Own Yorkshire Light Infantry Regiment take part in anti-aircraft practice with their Bren gun in the centre of the Burmese capital Rangoon. They are wearing khaki drill shirts and shorts with the India pattern cork sun helmet which was widely worn in Burma in 1941–2. In the background is the famous Schwe Dragon Pagoda, one of the most important Buddhist shrines in Burma.

Indian mountain artillerymen pose proudly with a Thompson sub-machine gun during an exercise in the hills of eastern Burma in 1941. They belong to the BFF which relied for many of its personnel on Indians rather than Burmese. The Thompson is an early model M1928 AI with a vertical fore grip and a large fifty-round drum magazine. This model is heavy and rather cumbersome for jungle fighting but the BFF would have been lucky to receive any due to demands from other fronts. In December 1941 all the BFF columns were supplied with five Thompsons and a single 2in mortar to improve their firepower.

Air Chief Marshal Sir Robert Brooke-Popham, Commander-in-Chief of the British Far East Command, in conference at his Singapore headquarters, December 1941. Brooke-Popham was soon replaced by General Wavell before the end of 1941 whose new command was known as the ABDA, or 'American-British-Dutch-Australian' Command. During his tenure Brooke-Popham had stated that there were no signs that the Japanese were going to invade anyone!

Indian dock workers un-crate a Blenhiem Mk IV medium bomber in Singapore before the outbreak of war with Japan. The defence of Malaya and Singapore would depend largely on the weak RAF forces stationed there. One notable mission that the Blenhiems undertook in 1941–2 was the bombing of Bangkok, capital of Thailand, in January 1941. Blenhiems were slow bombers and had been largely replaced in RAF service by 1942, although they continued to serve in the Far East until 1943.

Vickers M1912 machine-gunners of the Manchester Regiment take part in pre-war jungle training in Malaya in early 1941. The caption to this photograph sums up quite well the unrealistic view of the jungle-fighting capabilities of the British forces in 1941–2 in the Far East. It says that the Vickers 'is easily recognised because of its distinctive cooling drum, but an approaching enemy will not find it easy to spot the camouflaged gun team'. Unfortunately it was often the Allied troops who did not spot the Japanese troops' outflanking positions, like this one.

Volunteers of the Singapore Volunteer Corps leave their barracks to go to their jungle training camp in 1941. They have drawn from the unit armoury ammunition for their Lewis guns, a flare pistol and a Boys anti-tank rifle. Their khaki drill shirts and shorts and woollen socks are topped off with the archetypal cork solar topee. Webbing equipment is the older 1908 pattern no longer in service with the regular British army.

A two-man Indian crew of a Boys Mk I 0.55 anti-tank rifle in the Malayan jungle take part in firing practice in the months leading up to the start of the war against Japan. The Far East theatre was not given priority for weaponry and equipment before and after the outbreak of the war in 1939. For this reason this almost obsolete weapon would have been gratefully received by the Indians preparing to defend Malaya against possible Japanese aggression.

An Australian soldier demonstrates the anti-mosquito clothing and equipment which should have been available to all troops in Malaya. Although not very comfortable in the humid conditions, the net cover, long gloves and trousers tucked into his puttees provided protection. Malaria was to affect thousands of troops on both sides throughout the fighting in South-East Asia. The disease often resulted in units having to fight at well below full strength with a large proportion of these troops in the sick bay.

A 3in mortar crew of the Malay Regiment takes part in training during the summer of 1941. The Malay Regiment had been formed in March 1933 after the British had overcome their hesitance at arming Malays. By 1938 the regiment had a strength of 380 men which was further increased when war broke out in Europe in 1939. In February 1940 an additional company was added to the regiment and by July it had been merged with the 2nd Loyal Brigade. By 1941 the regiment was known as the 1st Malaya Brigade and by the time it took its defence positions in Singapore it had 1,400 men.

A column of Bren-gun carriers and light trucks of the Australian army moves across a bridge in Malaya in August 1941. The Bren-gun carrier was never intended to be a combat vehicle and had been designed to transport troops into battle. There were a number of this type of armoured vehicle in service in the Far East in 1941 but many ended up abandoned in Singapore. Officially, every British infantry battalion was supposed to have thirteen carriers but in 1941 few units had their full complement.

Australian troops march out of their barracks in Malaya to go on an exercise as they prepare for the expected war with Japan in 1941. In September 1939 the Australian government immediately declared war on Germany as part of the British Empire. Although the Australian Imperial Forces (AIF) were to play a crucial role in fighting in North Africa and the Far East, in 1939 they were ill prepared. With only 3,000 men in the regular army and with only 6 cruisers and 5 destroyers in its navy, rapid expansion of the armed forces was a priority. Within a year there were 40,000 additional soldiers trained including the 8th Division, which was despatched to help defend Malaya.

A QF 2-pounder anti-tank gun of the Australian army in Malaya has been sited on the edge of the jungle. It had already seen service with the Australians in the North African desert where its poor range meant it had to be dug in in order to be able to engage the enemy. During the fighting in Malaya the crews of the Australian 2-pounders were able to use their experience to successfully destroy a number of Japanese tanks.

Australian motorcycle despatch riders parade astride their Triumph 3SW motorcycles, one of several types used during 1941–2. Amongst the others were Norton, Indian, BSA and Aerial motorcycles, mostly imported from Britain. These men are amongst the Australian units that arrived in Malaya on 18 February 1941. They had plenty of time to acclimatize to the tropical conditions whilst some of their compatriots arrived at the end of the campaign.

Lewis light machine-gunners of the Straits Settlement Volunteer Force train during the months leading up to the Japanese invasion. In total there were 17,000 Malay volunteers of European, Eurasian or Asian ethnicity in December 1941. The two main forces were four battalions of the Straits Settlement Volunteers and four battalions of the Federated Malay States Volunteer Force. There was also a number of smaller volunteer units of infantry and light artillery in the other states of Malaya.

A line of recently arrived Marmon-Herrington Mk III MFF armoured cars wait to be assigned to their new units in Singapore in December 1941. By late November 1941 a total of 84 Marmon-Herrington armoured cars had been shipped to Malaya from South Africa. Some of these arrived just before the war broke out and their drivers had to be given a brief training course before going to the front. The Australian 8th Infantry Division and the 3rd Indian Cavalry Regiment were each given some of the more serviceable armoured cars.

This parade in August 1941 by the 2/15th Punjab Regiment is taking place in Kuching, the administrative capital of the British territory of Sarawak. It was organized to try and raise the profile of the Sarawak Volunteers, a local defence force, and stimulate recruitment. After an invasion scare in April 1941 the authorities in Labaun Island, Sarawak, Brunei and northern Borneo tried to build up their meagre defences. These four territories shared the vast island of Borneo with Dutch Borneo and were a real outpost of empire. Before the Japanese invaded in December 1941 an air-raid precautions unit and other civil defence groups had been formed. In addition an old para-military force, the Sarawak Rangers, had been re-formed mainly with older veterans. In December 1941 the garrison had a strength of 2,565 men, both regulars and volunteers, equipped with ten Bren-gun carriers, four 18-pounder field guns and a number of Boys anti-tank rifles and mortars.

New Guinean local forces were initially made up of the Papua Infantry Battalion, which started with 300 troops. These recruits are going through basic training in late 1941 in Port Moresby, the administrative capital of British New Guinea. In January 1942 this now expanded unit was the first to encounter the Japanese imperial forces when they landed on the island. Its 77 Australian officers and 550 other ranks held up the Japanese advance with a series of skilful ambushes and other surprise attacks.

Armed policemen of the Solomon Islands Protectorate Constabulary are seen on parade in 1941, when their force numbered 100 men. They, along with the Solomon Islands Defence Force, were responsible for protecting the various islands from the Japanese. The Defence Force, with a strength of 680 men, had been formed in 1939 but due to budget cuts was to be disbanded in February 1942. When the Japanese invaded the islands the disbandment had not taken place and most of the men served the Allied forces during the Solomons Campaign from 1942 onwards.

The crew of an anti-aircraft gun go through their drill in front of the public in Colombo, capital of Ceylon, in 1940. Ceylon was seen by the Japanese as a potential conquest as it would enable them to protect their position in the Indian Ocean. If they could invade Ceylon they would be able to use it as a base to totally disrupt any Allied shipping in the Indian Ocean. Any threat to Ceylon would come from the sea so there were four coastal batteries at Colombo and five at the main port of Trincomalee. During the war the garrison of Ceylon was made up of ten volunteer infantry battalions and four artillery regiments and was bolstered by British and Australian troops.

Chapter Three

'Defence on a Shoestring' – The Philippines Army, 1935–41

During the 1930s the Philippines underwent a process of transition which was to lead to its full independence from the USA by 1944. Ever since the military victory of the USA over the Philippines' former colonial masters, the Spanish, in 1898 the Americans had governed the islands. As far as the Filipinos were concerned, they had exchanged one colonial master for another and a vicious five-year-long guerrilla struggle against the US Army and Marines ensued. Like other South-East Asian colonies, the Philippines campaigned for a level of independence and by the 1930s the USA was ready to grant a phased independence. In 1934 the US and Filipino politicians signed a ten-year agreement which established a Philippines government. As part of the semi-independence of the Philippines a new National Army was to be formed. The Philippines National Defence Act of 1935 called for the setting up of a 10,000-strong regular army with a reserve force which was to reach 400,000 by 1946. It was intended that in time of war this fully trained reserve force could be mobilized quickly to defend the country. If all went according to plan this new army was proposed to be supported by at least 100 modern fast bombers and a fleet of fast patrol boats. A strong army, air force and navy was expected to be able to defend the Philippines from any aggressor without the assistance of the USA. There was no intention to create a military arm that could be used aggressively, this was to be a purely defensive force. This new National Army was, however, to face many difficulties, the main one being the size of its budget. It was supposed to operate on an austere 'shoestring' budget with every possible economy made regarding weaponry, equipment and uniforms. As the army developed its main ethos seemed to be to make sure that every single dollar was accounted for and no wastage was allowed. Artillery field guns were ex-US army cast-offs and its light guns were pre-1900 models. The National Army did have a few armoured cars and half-tracks but no tanks when the Japanese invaded in 1941. The first group of Filipino recruits for the National Army was called up on 1 January 1937 and by the end of 1939 there were 4,800 officers and 104,000 other ranks in the reserves. Training of the infantry recruits was split between a number of camps throughout the Philippines. Artillery training took place at Fort Stotsenburg to the north of Manila, whilst specialist training was given at Fort William McKinley to the south of the capital. A Philippines Army Air Corps took a while to get off the ground with the first military airfield just outside Manila having only three trainers. Older models of US planes were bought cheaply from the US air force and the air corps' main fighter in 1941 was totally obsolete. A training programme for pilots and ground crew took place exclusively in the USA in the late 1930s, and by 1940 the Army Air Corps had 40 planes and 100 pilots had been fully trained. Combat aircraft were at a premium with a squadron of twelve obsolete P-26 fighters and three worn-out B-10 medium bombers. There were also two P-12 fighters which had been bought in March 1940 for a 'very low price'.

Attempts were made before 1941 to improve the training and weaponry of the army by its commander US General Douglas MacArthur. His demands for newer equipment, including steel helmets for his men, came up constantly against the usual budgetary constraints. On 26 July 1941 the Philippines army was put under the command of the US army. The same day a new command was created by the US War Department named the 'US Forces in the Far East', or USAFE. This unified US-Philippines command was based in Manila under the leadership of General MacArthur. Little changed after July even though MacArthur tried his best to organize his large and unwieldy forces for the coming campaign.

In addition to the National Army there were also several existing armed formations in the Philippines pre-1941. There was the Philippines Scouts, which had first been recruited in 1899 to support the US army in its war against local guerrillas. During the early 1900s when the guerrilla threat was at its height it reached a strength of 71,000 but by the 1930s was acting as a local paramilitary police force. The Scouts were mainly absorbed into the 1st Philippines Division which was a regular formation of the US army and had a strength of 10,473 mixed Filipinos and Americans in December 1941. The 31st US Regiment, which was the only all-American formation in the Philippines in 1941, was included in the division too. There was also a paramilitary police force, the Philippines Constabulary (PC), which in 1940 had a strength of 7,000 men. Many of the PC were forced into one of the 10 National Army divisions hastily put together as the war with Japan loomed. When the Japanese invaded the National Army had 20,000 trained regulars and 100,000 untrained conscripts. Many of the new intake were illiterate and some could not understand the dialects of the officers issuing them with orders. Training of these scratch divisions varied from unit to unit and even the strength of each unit depended on where it was formed. In the general chaos of the Japanese invasion raw recruits were often sent into battle with no training whatsoever.

Soldiers of the Philippines National Army march through Manila on their first public parade in February 1937. The man given responsibility for the formation of the new National Army of the Philippines was General Douglas MacArthur. During the late 1930s and into 1941 he constantly tried to acquire more funding for the army which was run on a very tight budget.

This photograph taken in July 1941 shows a 155mm gun crew of the Philippines artillery going through a dummy drill on a piece of heavy artillery. At this stage the crew are having to simulate the drill as they do not have the shells to fire the gun, which is probably unsafe to use anyway.

Happy recruits of the Philippines army are about to take part in drill using wooden rifles in lieu of the real thing. The Philippines government had to arm their troops with the cheapest models of rifle and other weaponry. General MacArthur tried to modernize the Philippines army both in terms of its training and its weaponry and submitted a shopping list of equipment. He requested, amongst other items, 84,500 Garand M-1 rifles, 656 light and heavy machine guns, 450 37mm anti-tank guns, 217 81mm mortars and 288 75mm field guns. In addition, he asked for the army to be supplied with 120,000 steel helmets of the First World War variety.

Philippines army recruits undergo basic training at Fort McKinley in March 1941. One of the half a dozen camps used for that purpose, McKinley was also used to train the more able recruits in specialized roles such as communications, engineering and motorized warfare. These men are armed with the Springfield M1903 rifle rather than the Enfield P-17 which was the standard model in service with the Philippines military. In view of the poor budget for the army, the price of 18 pesos per P-17 compared too favourably with the 65 pesos that the USA wanted for the Springfield.

Two tribesmen turn up at a recruiting office of the Philippines National Army in the summer of 1941. They appear to be arousing some interest from the other recruits who are Westernized city dwellers. One of the weaknesses of the Philippines army was the number of dialects spoken by its troops, who were recruited from a range of diverse backgrounds. Many did not understand either English or Spanish or the most common Philippines language, Tagalog. This lack of a common language was of course a major problem for the army officers, most of whom came from urban areas.

A 37mm anti-tank gun is operated by its crew, of the Philippines Scouts, on a pre-war manoeuvre. The Philippines Scouts had been formed in 1899 to support the US army fighting against the nationalists. The unit had maintained a good reputation for over forty years and in 1941 MacArthur wanted to expand it into a much large formation. It was suggested that reservists for the Philippines Army were used, as well as suitable civilians. Any applicant had to have the right aptitude to join what was considered an elite unit and be aged between 20 and 28 years old.

A 75mm M1917 gun crew of the 1st Philippines Division takes part in training in the months before the outbreak of war. The Philippines army was desperately short of artillery with what guns that were available having to be shared out amongst the various commands. When war broke out the 11th and 21st Artillery Regiments did not receive their 75mm field guns until 8 December. They were luckier than the artillery element of the Visayan-Mindanao Force whose guns went down with the SS *Corriegidor* which sank on 17 December having hit a mine.

This T 7 scout car belongs to the headquarters troop of the mechanized unit of the 26th Cavalry of the Philippines Scouts. It is taking part in a pre-war manoeuvre in the last few days before the Japanese attacked Pearl Harbor. The Philippines Scouts was the elite unit of the Philippines Division and was to be used by the USA to bolster the rest of the army during 1941–2. Although bristling with three machine guns and Thompson sub-machine guns, this overcrowded armoured car, first built in 1934, would be a sitting duck if used in combat in this way.

A medical unit of the Philippines army uses an unusual form of transport for an injured soldier – his stretcher is being pulled by a water buffalo. The Philippines military had constantly to cut corners as its low budget did not allow for large numbers of motor vehicles. Presumably buffalo were much cheaper to run and maintain than conventional ambulances.

This photograph of Philippines army recruits shows the uniform worn during the 1930s and until 1942 by the ordinary Filipino soldier to good effect. The uniform was quite basic with a cotton shirt and shorts worn with a fairly cheap pair of canvas shoes. There were no overcoats or cold weather clothing included in the issue uniforms and presumably the soldiers were not expected to be on duty during cold Philippines nights. Shoes wore out quickly and new issues of replacements were sporadic as the logistics department had to keep to a tight budget.

In this photograph of a heavy machine-gun unit with Browning .30 calibre M1917 medium machine guns we can see another item of uniform, the 'guinit' helmet. The varnished guinit helmet was made from coconut fibre and looked like a standard colonial cork solar topee. Although the helmets worn by these men are in good condition, it appears that this item was prone to go out of shape when in service. Another disadvantage with the helmet was that the varnish it was coated with often caught the sun and gave away the wearer's position. Its only advantage as far as the Philippines army was concerned was that it was cheaper than a steel helmet.

Philippines army recruits take part in training wearing their gas masks, which following policy were almost certainly made locally. The army wore equipment and uniforms that were almost totally made in the Philippines using local products. Belts were produced from abaca instead of canvas and the buttons on the shirt were created from coconut shells. Other locally made items of uniform and equipment were a pair of white socks, a blanket and a mosquito net. A fatigue uniform made from blue denim worn with rubber shoes was sometimes worn for front-line duty in 1941–2.

Recruits go through physical training wearing the blue-denim trousers from their fatigue uniforms in early 1941. They are all using their Enfield P-17 rifles as part of the training in an attempt to build up the soldiers' stamina. Like other Asian soldiers, most Filipinos were of slighter build and European rifles like the P-17 were cumbersome to use. In order to allow the expansion of the Philippines army the US loaned them some extra rifles as the budget would not stretch to buying them.

In a pre-war demonstration Philippines army crews of the 23rd Field Artillery fire their QF 2.95in Vickers-Maxim mountain gun. This elderly field piece was a leftover from the late 1800s/early 1900s campaigns of the US army. Although outdated, the gun could fire its 12.5lb shell to a range of 4,825yd and could be broken down into four mule loads. Regardless of its failings, the mountain gun was all that the Philippines army had available to supplement their 75mm field gun.

These Filipino nurses are participating in firing practice with target rifles as part of their training in 1941. The Philippines Army Nurse Corps had been formed in 1940 and the first fifty-eight nurses were appointed in August of that year. In the patriarchal society of the Philippines women's roles in the military were always going to be limited. However, women did make significant contributions to the anti-Japanese guerrilla movement from 1942 until 1945, even commanding some groups.

Chapter Four

'The Forgotten Army' – The Army of the Netherlands East Indies, 1941

When the Netherlands was invaded and occupied by the German army in May 1940 some politicians escaped from the country to form a new government in exile in London. The Dutch Queen Wilhelmina also escaped to London and immediately allied her government in exile with the British and after December 1941 with the USA. Although the Netherlands itself may have fallen, the government in London still controlled the vast Dutch possessions in the Far East as well as Surinam in South America and several other small territories. To defend the Netherlands East Indies (modern Indonesia) the Dutch had the Koninklijk Nederlands Indisch Leger, or Netherlands Army in the East Indies. Commonly known as the Netherlands East Indies Army, or abbreviated simply as the KNIL, it had a strength of about 70,000 men. It was made up largely of local native recruits who often served in units with European NCOs and even recruits. It was backed up by a second-line formation known as the Stadswacht which included just about every able-bodied Dutch male. Some of the native soldiers of the KNIL were regarded as being unreliable which further weakened the cohesion of the army's units, especially those with mixed troops in them. The KNIL did have some light tanks, artillery and anti-aircraft guns but not in the quantities needed for a modern mechanized army. Attempts by the Dutch government in exile to purchase additional armaments were fraught with difficulty. They did place large orders including one for 600 light tanks from the USA, but only 7 arrived in time to fight the Japanese. Most available arms suppliers were already selling everything they had to one side or the other in Europe. The KNIL even resorted to placing adverts in US newspapers looking to buy machine guns in private collectors' hands! This desperate search for new weapons saw a wide variety of sub-machine guns and machine guns used by the KNIL. With all the difficulties facing it there was little expectation that the KNIL would be able to resist a Japanese invasion. One commentator dismissed the KNIL as an 'internal security constabulary' rather than a modern army.

It was true that the KNIL had been distributed throughout the Netherlands East Indies in small company or battalion size garrisons. Inter arm training and military exercises were also rare and until the war began regimental headquarters had been purely administrative. Essentially, the KNIL, although more than willing to fight, was not equipped or trained to face the kind of ruthless foe they were about to meet. Attempts had been made at modernizing the KNIL including the formation of an armoured unit on the island of Java. This mobile column was made up of a tank company with three seven-tank platoons equipped with a mixture of Cardon-Lloyd M1936s and Marmon-Herrington CTLS light tanks. Both of these types of tanks were lightly armoured and poorly armed but were of similar quality to the Japanese light tanks. In addition the column had a HQ platoon with three M1936s, a reconnaissance platoon with three Marmon-Herringtons and a mechanized infantry company. This was equipped with sixteen Braat armoured personnel carriers produced on Java in local workshops.

At the start of the fighting in early 1942 the KNIL and other armed formations in the Netherlands East Indies totalled 122,600 men. These comprised 45,800 Europeans (including 12,100 regulars) and 55,600 native troops (28,200 regulars) along with 7,600 militia and 8,500 short-term conscripts. Second-line formations included the Stadswachten with 8,500 Europeans and the Landwachten with 19,000 mixed native and European volunteers. In addition to the army there was also the air arm known as the Militaire Luchtvaart van het Koninklijk Nederlands-Indisch Leger (ML-KNIL) with about 316 aircraft including 130 fighters and 30 heavy bombers. Many of the ML-KNIL's aircraft were outdated or simply worn out despite the best efforts of the Dutch government in exile to purchase more modern planes. The Dutch Royal Navy in the East Indies had 5 light cruisers, 8 destroyers, 15 sbmarines and a number of smaller vessels. Most of these ships were to see service in the defence of the Netherlands East Indies and few were to survive the sea battles of 1942 (see Chapter Twelve).

KNIL soldiers on an assault course at Bandoeng, Java in February 1941. The rather outdated uniform worn by the men is indicative of the KNIL. Although the KNIL had seen extensive service against local rebellions during the nineteenth and early twentieth centuries, it was ill prepared for the total war it would soon have to face.

KNIL troops move through the barbed wire obstacle course as part of their basic training in Java. The majority of KNIL troops were native recruits raised from certain regions and tribes of Indonesia. Some regions were in almost constant rebellion against Dutch rule and the men of those islands and provinces were rarely recruited to serve in the KNIL. These European recruits are armed with the Mannilicher M95 rifle which was standard in the Dutch army in 1940 and the KNIL in 1941–2.

A bugler of the KNIL is seen in a pre-war parade wearing the typical green cotton uniform. The headgear is the archetypal rattan hat with the brim worn down instead of pinned up at the side with a metal tricolour roundel. Native recruits for the KNIL came unsurprisingly from regions that were pro-Dutch rather than from regions such as Acteh on the island of Sumatra that were in regular revolt.

The native crew of a KNIL Bofors 40mm anti-aircraft gun operates the gun by listening to the aimer's instructions through ear phones. All the crewmen wear the M1928 steel helmet with the leather sunscreen fastened to its rear. There were two modern medium anti-aircraft guns in KNIL service, the forty-six Bofors 40mm and thirty-two 75mm Model 1929s made by the same manufacturer. Dutch purchasers asked for the calibre of the guns to be increased slightly to 80mm and these modified guns were given the designation M/36. With only thirty-two of the 80mm guns in the KNIL armoury in 1941–2 these had to sited at the most strategic targets.

The KNIL crew of a Flak 30 20mm anti-aircraft gun takes part in a pre-war practice on Java. A number of these modern German guns which were manufactured by Rheinmetall were sold to the KNIL in 1939. They were the main light anti-aircraft gun in service in 1941–2 but there were only thirty available in 1942. They were supplemented by 140 12.7mm colt heavy machine guns, many of which were mounted on the backs of trucks. To increase the mobility of the Flak 30 they were supposed to be towed by Vickers Utility tractors which also carried the crews.

This KNIL anti-aircraft gunner is operating a primitive acoustic sound locater which was used to pinpoint enemy aircraft. The Dutch government sent six of this type of listening equipment to the Netherlands East Indies in 1936. It was a cheaper alternative to the larger types in use with European armies but was out of date by 1941. Operators found it difficult to locate and track the faster aircraft which had come into service in the early 1940s.

A tractor pulls a KNIL field howitzer up a slope during a field training exercise in 1941. The gun is a Swedish-made Bofors 105mm M1924 field howitzer which was to supplement the Bofors 75mm M1924. There were fourteen of the 105mm and twenty-eight of the 75mm in KNIL service and these were used alongside older guns. Dutch-made copies of the Krupp 75mm also saw service with the KNIL artillery and thirty-four of the Siderius M1911 were in use in 1942. Another thirty-six were slightly modified M1911/33s with were also used by the KNIL during the 1942 fighting.

This KNIL crew of an Austrian-made 4.7cm Bohler anti-tank gun are a mix of European and Indonesian personnel. The gun, which was known as the Kanon van 4.7, in Dutch service was not a particularly good anti-tank weapon. It should, however, have been able to deal with all types of tank in service with the Japanese in 1941. There were a total of 72 of these guns in service with the KNIL in 1941–2. The gun crew are all armed with the M95 carbine which was used by cavalrymen as well as artillery crews.

The KNIL crew of a Bofors 105mm field howitzer fire their gun in a pre-war field exercise. This Swedish gun was designed for the commercial market by Bofors and equipped two KNIL artillery regiments. In common with most KNIL heavy equipment and weaponry, the guns were divided up amongst the various garrisons making them largely ineffective. Like the artillery crews of many nations, some KNIL gun crews battled to the last man when the fighting with Japan began.

A native soldier of the KNIL fires a British-produced Vickers M1912 heavy machine gun. The Vickers has a bamboo frame around its water jacket to allow it to be carried without burning the gun crew. There were about 1,000 of this type of heavy machine gun in service with the KNIL during the 1941–2 campaign. The soldier's hat is the green painted rattan type worn by most KNIL troops alongside the Dutch M1928 steel helmet.

Young native troops of the KNIL march past the cathedral in Batavia, the administrative capital of Java, in late 1941. Amongst the units of the KNIL there were a number of independent regiments, battalions and legions of various size raised by local sultans in Java. This was similar to the system in British India where local sultans, maharajahs and other rulers raised their own units which in times of war served as part of the Indian army. These Dutch units were part of the KNIL defence forces in 1942 and wore the same uniform with their own distinct badges. Amongst the so-called detached units were the 'Korps Barisan', which had three battalions, and the battalion-sized 'Korps Prajoda'. There was also the battalion-sized 'Legion Mangkoe Negoro' and the company sized 'Legion Pakoe Alam'.

A unit of the Stadwacht takes part in a parade on Java in the build up to the Japanese invasion in early 1942. The shortage of modern weapons in the Netherlands East Indies meant that some volunteers had to be armed with whatever was available. This included the C-96 automatic pistol, which could be bought from a number of manufacturers in Europe. Volunteers usually came from the older generation, reserved occupations and younger men who were not fit enough to soldier full time. Some Stadwacht units such as those from Batavia, Bandoeng, Sematang and Algemeen had their own distinctive tin badges which they wore on their left breast.

A native soldier of the KNIL is seen with his unique weaponry in about 1940. He has a Mannlicher M1895 carbine tucked under his left arm and a Klewang fighting sword in his right hand. The Klewang was a weapon that originated in the East Indies in the late 1800s and was adopted by the KNIL. It was intended as a close-quarter sword to be employed in the jungle and troops were given specialist training in its use.

In a pre-war demonstration of the KNIL's armoured 'might' a unit of Cardon-Lloyd M1936s charges across a paddy field. In 1936 twenty-four of these British-made light tanks were purchased by the KNIL, but many were worn out by 1942. Most of the survivors were formed with other armoured vehicles into a mobile column just before the war. Light tanks like this had already been declared obsolete in other armies apart from in the Japanese Imperial Army.

A line of Braat Overwalwagens, armed with two machine guns, one at the front and one at the rear, are seen in Java before the fighting began. Because there were few armoured vehicles available on the world market after 1939 the KNIL decided to produce some of its own. There were three different models of the Braat, and the Stadwacht model, seen here, was used by the Home Guard. The two other versions were an anti-aircraft model with heavy machine guns fitted and a 'patrol car' version with four Madsen machine guns.

A line of KNIL soldiers are seen on parade in 1941 wearing their distinctive dark-green uniform. It was basically the same design as that worn by the Netherlands army in 1940 but was made from lightweight material. Equipment is standard Dutch army issue with brown leather belts and ammunition pouches. The rattan hat was obviously meant to shade the wearer from the sun and the brim on the right side could be worn down or pinned up.

A native soldier of the KNIL displays one of the types of sub-machine gun in service in 1941–2. The Dutch government in exile had great difficulty in finding weapons to arm the KNIL with after 1940. With the world at war from 1939 there were few arms manufacturers that could supply them. This MP-28/II sub-machine gun along with the similar MP-34 had, however, been ordered from Germany in 1938.

KNIL mountain artillery move their gun on pack animals across a stream during a pre-war exercise. The mixed native and European crew are wearing the M1928 steel helmet with a leather sun shield added at the back. Most of them are armed with Mannlicher M1895 carbines but the man in the foreground has a M.39 sub-machine gun. This was the Dutch designation for the MP-28/II which entered service with the KNIL in 1939.

Chapter Five

The Japanese Empire Versus the USA – 'Japan Strikes, 1941'

The Japanese Empire appeared to be heading towards war with the USA throughout 1941 and there did not seem to be anything that could be done to stop this. Japanese planners realized that the USA and its navy would be the main threat to its 'Southern Road' doctrine in the Pacific. Although the Royal Navy was the premier naval power, its resources were stretched throughout the world and it had little presence in the Far East and Pacific. Throughout 1941 the USA and Japan were engaged in intensive negotiations to try and resolve their differences. The USA insisted that Japan should make peace with Chiang Kai-shek's China and eventually withdraw from the country. On their side the Japanese insisted that the USA must stop its economic sanctions against them and recognize their dominance of eastern Asia. In October 1941 the rise to power of General Tojo more or less ended any serious discussion and the intransigence on both sides grew deeper.

Japanese naval planners, meanwhile, had been deciding how best to try and overcome the US navy's pre-eminence in the Pacific. Most realized that in a long-lasting conflict the USA's much larger industrial capacity would ensure its eventual victory. They thought that the only way to counter this advantage was to launch a pre-emptive strike against the US Pacific Fleet. Originally, they had planned to destroy the US fleet at sea as it sailed to bring reinforcements to the various places that the Imperial Army was planning to attack in late 1941. Imperial Navy task forces would wait for the Imperial Army's ground attacks on Malaya, Burma and the Philippines. Then when the US Pacific Fleet sailed to relieve the Allied forces defending these territories the massed Japanese fleet would strike and destroy their rivals in one mammoth naval battle in the Philippine Sea. Admiral Yamamoto, the chief Japanese naval strategist, knew that the only possible way to swing the balance in favour of the Imperial Fleet was to change the plan around. His ships would launch a pre-emptive strike against the US Pacific Fleet before war was officially declared. If this strike was successful it would allow the Japanese Imperial Army to conquer Burma, Malaya, the Philippines and the Netherlands East Indies. Once all these objectives had been achieved the Japanese would be able to negotiate a peace with the USA favourable to them. Yamamoto was realistic about the odds stacked against the Imperial Navy and quietly voiced his reservations to colleagues. He was pro-American and had spent time in the USA and admired the country and spoke candidly to two of his trusted aides: 'Gentlemen you know I'm against the war with the United States. But I am an officer of the Imperial Navy and a subject of his Majesty the Emperor. Recent international events and developments here at home, make such a war seem almost inevitable, and it is my duty as Commander in Chief to be ready'.

Despite the reservations of Yamamoto and other navy and army officers, the plans for war with the USA continued. By mid-November the war was seen as inevitable and the plans for the attack on the US navy's base, Pearl Harbor in the Hawaiian Islands, were put in motion. The Japanese Imperial Navy's task force, which sailed out of its bases on 26 November heading into the Pacific, was made up of six aircraft carriers, the *Akagi, Kaga, Shokaku, Zuikaku, Hiryu* and *Soryu*. These carriers had 423 aircraft between them, up to 360 of which were to be used in the attack on Pearl Harbor. They were escorted by 2 battleships, 2 heavy cruisers, 9 destroyers and 3 submarines, which were to be refuelled by 8 tankers. Their main target was the 4 US navy aircraft carriers and 8 to 9 battleships which they expected to be moored in Pearl Harbor when they struck. If the element of surprise was achieved, the destruction of the US fleet would give the Japanese dominance in the Western Pacific for many months.

Whilst the Japanese fleet was at sea a meeting of the Japanese Imperial Conference ratified the plan and gave it the go-ahead. The Japanese managed to get to their strike positions undiscovered by Friday, 5 December and the final order to attack was given. At 6.00 am on Sunday, 7 December the first of two strikes went in and the first bombs were dropped at 7.55 am. The US battleships were neatly lined up in the harbour and most were hit by bombs and struck with torpedoes. For the Japanese the attack was a great success but the expected US carriers were not at Pearl Harbor, but on manoeuvres at sea. In addition, the fuel dumps which should have been destroyed were not targeted and a third air attack never took place. Material losses for the US navy were 8 battleships sunk or badly damaged and 3 cruisers, 3 destroyers, 2 auxiliary ships and 2 smaller vessels sunk. Aircraft losses on the ground totalled 188 with few planes able to get airborne during the attacks. Although the human losses were disputed, after the war the US navy admitted 2,330 dead and 1,347 wounded; 1,000 of the dead were crewmen cruelly trapped beneath decks on the battleship USS *Arizona*. The US government declared war on Japan on 8 December, as did the British government. In the meantime, the Japanese had launched their ground offensive in Malaya and were about to invade the Philippines and several US-controlled Pacific Islands.

Once the Pearl Harbor attack was underway the US Pacific Islands immediately became a target for the Japanese. The various US Pacific Islands garrisons were made up mainly of small US marine units, which in 1940 were organized into defence battalions. By 1941 there were 7 defence battalions with the 1st Unit divided between atolls close to Hawaii and Wake Island. The 2nd Defence Battalion garrisoned American

Samoa where it was supported by the 1st Samoa Battalion raised from US marine reservists in August 1941. There was also a small 'Fita-Fita' Guard which was locally raised and had a strength of about 100 men. Midway Island, one of the most isolated US Pacific Islands, was garrisoned by the 3rd Defence Battalion, and was eventually joined by the 6th Unit. A 7th Defence Battalion reinforced the 2nd Battalion in American Samoa.

Guam was defended in December 1941 by a force of 153 US marines and 271 sailors and naval personnel. In addition, there were 134 construction workers who could be armed and 247 local militia and the Guam Insular Forces Guard. All the local forces were under the command of Chief Petty Officer Lane and wore surplus US navy white uniforms. Although willing to fight, the Insular Guard was poorly trained and like the rest of the garrison had no heavy weaponry. It had a total of 3 Lewis light machine guns, 4 Thompson sub-machine guns and 85 Springfield M1903 rifles. The Japanese attacking Guam on 9 December totalled 5,900, comprising the 400-strong 5th Defence Force from Saipan and the 5,500-strong South Seas Detachment. This overwhelming force was resisted manfully by the US and local forces for a couple of days. With odds of nearly 100 to 1, the end result was beyond doubt and was followed by a cruel occupation from which the native Chamorro population was to suffer terribly until 1945.

Wake Island had a garrison of 400 US marines in August 1941 who had arrived there without much of their arms and equipment. They had little in the way of heavy weaponry and the barbed wire they needed to build the islands defences did not turn up either. On 4 December the island did receive twelve Grumman Wildcat fighters of the Marines VMF-211 Squadron. These were flown in from the USS *Enterprise* raising the total US personnel on Wake to 449 including pilots and ground crew. Most of the Wake defenders were tied up manning the island's 5in guns and machine guns with only eighty-five men available to act as an infantry force to counter the Japanese landings. A Japanese naval task force appeared off Wake Island on 11 December and got a nasty surprise when the defenders fought them off. The marines even managed to sink two of the Japanese destroyers making up the task force, resulting in the invasion force and its 450-strong landing force having to withdraw temporarily. When the Japanese returned on 22 December they were far better prepared and had brought a much larger armada to overcome the few hundred defenders. This force included 2 aircraft carriers, 2 heavy cruisers and escorting destroyers and landing ships with about 2,000 men aboard. By 11.30 am on 23 December the brave resistance of the Wake Island defenders was over and they had to surrender.

Elsewhere the Japanese were beginning other attacks as their offensive got into full swing in Malaya and the Philippines.

On a US Pacific island the gun crew of a heavy anti-aircraft gun goes through a drill as tensions between the USA and the Japanese Empire rose. From 1940 until December 1941 the number of marines garrisoning the many islands controlled by the US in the Pacific was steadily increased. The few hundred men who made up most of these island garrisons were expected to hold back any attackers until assistance could arrive. Japanese planners had no intention of allowing the status quo to continue in the Pacific, however. In many cases no help was forthcoming and island defence battalions were left to fend for themselves.

A marine machine-gun crew are operating a Browning M1917 machine gun on an unidentified Pacific Island before the outbreak of war with Japan. The crew are wearing their khaki drill uniforms with their cork sun helmets whilst the officer wears a marine peaked cap. Several Pacific Islands such as Wake and Guam depended on a few hundred marines to defend them in 1941. Although small garrisons could inflict some casualties amongst the invading Japanese troops, without support they could only hold out for a few days.

A US 75mm M1897-A4 field gun fires from the beach near Honolulu on the Pacific island of Hawaii during the summer of 1941. The gun is on a modified M2A2 carriage with pneumatic tyres which had been added during the 1930s. At this stage the US army was still reliant to a large degree on these guns which had been used by the American Expeditionary Corps in France from 1917 to 1918. They were being phased out of service but many had to be used as a stop gap when the fighting began in December 1941.

A crewman of a 75mm field gun of the Philippines Division goes through practice drill in the year leading up to the outbreak of war. The Philippines Division was part of the regular US army but was recruited from the Filipino population. It had a strength of 10,473 men and had a good reputation compared with its Philippines army counterparts. Unfortunately, during the 1941–2 fighting it was not allowed to operate as a single unit and its men were split up into smaller groups which affected cohesion and performance.

The crew of a US T3 four-horn sound locator M1927 operates its early warning system in the hills of the Philippines in early 1941. This archaic-looking piece of machinery is typical of those used by the Japanese, French, British and Germans. Although it looks like some kind of gigantic gramophone, this kind of anti-aircraft equipment was vital in the days before radar. The Japanese equivalent to the T3 looked like the brass section of an orchestra but was still in use in 1942.

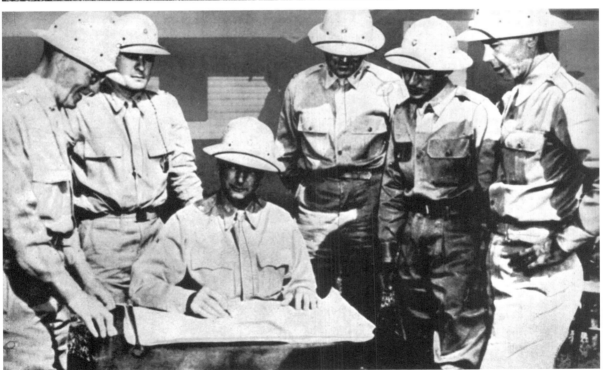

Lieutenant General Jonathan Wainwright seen in happier pre-1941 days with his staff wearing their tropical uniforms in his office in Manila. Wainwright was to go on to command the four-division strong North Luzon Force during the Philippines Campaign. He had been in the Philippines since 1940 having seen action there in the early 1900s as a young officer. His only other combat experience had been as a staff officer on the Western Front from 1917 to 1918.

US Air Force Douglas B-18 'Bolo' medium bombers fly in formation over the Hawaiian Islands in late 1940. The obsolete B-18 was still in service with some US squadrons in December 1941 even though its top speed of 216mph made it 'easy meat' for Japanese fighters. First ordered into production in 1936, the B-18 had a rather short service as a front-line bomber. Although most were destroyed in the 1941 Japanese attacks on Pearl Harbor and the Philippines, a few went on to give service as coastal patrol aircraft. The silver painted planes carry the pre-war US air force markings in bright red, white and blue.

Admiral Isoruku Yamamoto (1889–1943) pores over a map for the news cameraman in the build up to Pearl Harbor. Yamamoto was the architect of 'Z Plan' which called for the pre-emptive strike on Pearl Harbor, the US navy's Pacific base on Hawaii. He was made commander of the Japanese combined fleet in 1940 and was then able to push for Z Plan. Although the attack on the US naval base at Pearl Harbor was a naval victory, it was politically disastrous for Japan. The Japanese miscalculation was that the USA would eventually negotiate with a nation which had attacked it without a declaration of war. Japan had a history of pre-emptive strikes having attacked the Imperial Russian Fleet at Port Arthur in 1904. This naval attack began the Russo-Japanese War 1904–5 in which Yamamoto served as a junior officer.

One of the nasty surprises that the Allies had to face in 1941–2 was the carrier based fighter, the Mitsubishi A6M Zero or 'Zeke'. It was a lightly built and efficient fighter with a top speed of 316mph, was highly manoeuvrable and armed with 20mm cannons. During the early part of the Pacific War it swept the skies clear of Allied opposition leading the Japanese people to believe it was invincible. The Allies should not have been surprised by its performance as pilots of the American Volunteer Group had encountered it over China. Their intelligence reports about the Zero's capabilities were, however, not passed on to the correct authorities. If they had have been then the panic that many Allied pilots experienced when they fought it might have been lessened.

Japanese pilots gather in front of the tactical blackboard beneath decks on one of the aircraft carriers en route to Pearl Harbor. They are listening to the final instructions for the attack from their commanding officer and the ship's captain. These pilots did not think that Japan had any choice but to make a pre-emptive strike on the US Pacific Fleet. In their eyes the US, British and Dutch 'unjust' freezing of Japan's assets in July 1941 in protest at their continuing war in China was almost like a declaration of war. Without the ability to import oil it was only a matter of months before the Japanese economy and its war effort totally collapsed. This meant that any aggression by the Japanese Empire against the Western powers in the Far East and the Pacific was in their eyes defensive.

Japanese planes on the deck of the aircraft carrier *Hiryu* get ready to take off for the attack on Pearl Harbor. The aircraft in the foreground is a Mitsubishi A6M Zero fighter which provided protection for the Japanese attack. Behind the Zero is a Nakajima B5N which came in two models, a dive-bomber and a light bomber. During the first wave of the attacks on Pearl Harbor there were 51 Aichi D3A1 dive-bombers, 49 Nakajima B5N light bombers, 40 B5N2 dive-bombers and 43 Zero fighters involved.

In a scene similar to that in the previous photograph, the Japanese propaganda cameraman has taken a picture of a full flight deck onboard the aircraft carrier *Akagi*. There are several rows of A6M Zero fighters ready to take off with the rest of the deck covered in torpedo bombers. The two main types of carrier bombers engaged at Pearl Harbor were the Nakajima B5N2 'Kate' torpedo bomber and the Aichi D3A1 'Val' dive-bomber. Aichi D3A1s sank more Allied shipping than any other Axis dive-bomber never mind Japanese bombers during the war.

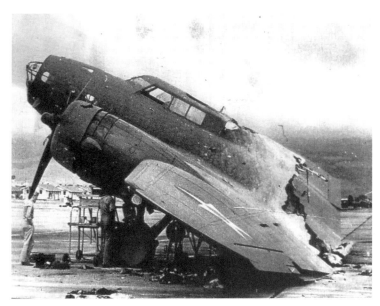

A B-17D heavy bomber lies with its back broken on Hickman airfield on the Hawaiian island of Oahu. There were twelve B-17Ds at Hickman and the Japanese destroyed five and damaged the remaining aircraft. In total the Japanese destroyed 188 US aircraft and damaged a further 159 on Oahu Island. Significantly, for the future US war effort the majority of these planes such as the P-36 fighter were bordering on obsolescence. The loss of the B-17s was a major blow but even these were the early model of the heavy bomber. New improved B-17s were to prove vital to the eventual US victory in the Pacific War from 1942–5.

Three civilians lie dead in their car which was targeted by a Japanese fighter as it flew over Pearl Harbor. Although the Japanese concentrated on military targets for obvious reasons, any people in a moving vehicle could become potential victims. In total sixty-eight civilians were killed and thirty-five wounded during the attacks on Pearl Harbor. Some were killed accidentally by US anti-aircraft artillery and some died as a result of unexploded anti-aircraft shells falling to earth and exploding in residential areas.

The USS *Arizona*, seen in the aftermath of the attack on Pearl Harbor, was the only battleship which was left beyond repair. Her magazine took a direct hit and exploded causing catastrophic damage and trapping most of the crew below decks. There was no chance to escape the *Arizona* as the battleship sank immediately taking 1,000 of its crew down with her. Nearly half of the casualties in the Pearl Harbor attack came from the *Arizona* whilst other ships' crews did manage to get off their stricken vessels.

The USS *West Virginia* burns whilst fire crews prepare to pull alongside in a futile effort to control the inferno. In total 19 US navy ships including 8 battleships were damaged or sunk and 2,403 crewmen were killed. Unfortunately for the Japanese, the three US Pacific Fleet aircraft carriers were at sea when they launched their attack. Attempts by Japanese reconnaissance planes to locate the carriers failed and they were forced to return home having only achieved part of their mission.

Sailors lay wreaths on the graves of their comrades in the days after the attack on Pearl Harbor. The sheer outrage felt by the US navy and the whole of the American population about the unprovoked attack on Pearl Harbor was palpable. Isolationists like Charles Lindbergh were silenced by the manner of the Japanese attack and most anti-war campaigners now joined the call for revenge. Admiral Yamamoto and most of his fellow officers had expected the USA to be incensed and fully anticipated that Japan would now have to 'reap the whirlwind'.

A two-man Japanese midget submarine lies washed up on an Hawaiian beach after failing in its mission at Pear Harbor. Five of these submarines had been carried to Pearl Harbor aboard some of the sixteen Imperial submarines which were part of the attack force. The intention was that these midget submarines would enter Pearl Harbor and attack simultaneously with the air strikes. Meanwhile, the full-size submarines were to scout for the carrier force and search for any US ships that managed to escape the attack. The midget submarine attack was one of the few failures of the Japanese plan and all of the vessels were unable to achieve their objectives.

Seven of Wake Island's twelve Wildcat fighters lie destroyed on the airfield after a Japanese bombing raid on 8 December. The Grumman F4-F Wildcats had arrived on the strategically important US island on 4 December. After the first air raid on the island, twenty-three of the fifty-five personnel of the Marine Air Squadron VMF-211 were dead. Another eleven of the squadron were wounded which meant that the Japanese now had almost total air superiority. The Japanese returned on 9 December but were shocked to be faced by the remaining four Wildcats which somehow had been put back into action. When the Japanese bombers left the island they had lost several of their aircraft shot down by the Wildcats and ground fire.

Japanese troops prepare to attack US defensive positions on the island of Guam after striking on 10 December. Guam, with its garrison of 271 naval personnel, 153 US marines, 80 locally recruited Insular Guard and 246 militia, could not hold for long. It was attacked by a total of 5,900 Japanese naval landing troops who were faced with militia armed only with rifles and a few machine guns. After a 2-hour battle the Guam commander navy Captain George McMillin decided to surrender the island to avoid civilian casualties. US losses during the fighting were nineteen killed and forty-two wounded, whilst the Japanese took the island suffering only ten casualties.

Chapter Six

'For Reasons of Prestige' –
The Fall of Hong Kong, 1941

To the people of the British Crown Colony of Hong Kong in southern China the Japanese attack on Pearl Harbor meant that an invasion would soon follow. Hong Kong had been a British possession since the late 1800s and besides the island of Hong Kong itself there were also the Leased Territories on the Chinese mainland including the port of Kowloon. The Japanese invasion of northern China in 1937 had been followed a year later by the takeover of the southern Chinese provinces to the north of Hong Kong. Whilst Britain and Japan were at peace Hong Kong might feel threatened but the Japanese dared not invade. Any prospective defence of the colony against the Japanese was downplayed by the British and Hong Kong was given little significance in the great scheme of things in war-torn Britain. There was a faint hope that Hong Kong might be able to defend itself for ninety days until reinforcements could arrive but this was wishful thinking. In 1940 Hong Kong was described anyway by British officials as 'an outpost of non-strategic importance'. The British Army Chief of Staff said that the colony was 'an undesirable military commitment'. He said that that only reason that they could not withdraw from Hong Kong was the loss of prestige that this action would cause for the British Empire. Hong Kong did have great importance as a trading post with China in peacetime but the Japanese occupation meant that it was at least temporarily of little use.

The problem with Hong Kong, as one commentator said, was that it was 'too far away from the British base at Singapore and it was too close to Japanese-ruled Formosa and a large bomber force [stationed there]'. In 1941 there were nearly 2 million civilians crammed into the small colony with the vast majority of the population being Chinese. There was also quite a large international community of foreign businessmen, bankers and their families in Hong Kong along with the long-standing expatriate British community.

The exact numbers of troops in the garrison is difficult to ascertain and different authors estimate it at between 10,000 and 14,000 men. It was made up of a mixture of British, Indians, Canadians and local volunteers and was not really a cohesive unit. With this ad-hoc group of units and part-units Hong Kong could not be successfully defended for long. The garrison was made up of the 2nd Battalion Royal Scots, the 1st Battalion of the Middlesex Regiment, 1st Battalion of the Winnipeg Rifles and one of the Royal Rifles of Canada. Indian troops in Hong Kong were from the 2/14 Battalion of Punjabis and the 5/7 Battalion of Rajputs. In their support were the 2,000 or so members of the Hong Kong Volunteers, who although not well trained put up a good fight alongside the regulars.

There was also a large number of Chinese Triad volunteers who were occupied mainly in hunting down a number of 'fifth columnists' who were reported to be helping the Japanese. These 'Loyal and Righteous' Chinese volunteers numbered at least 15,000 men and were more than willing to fight in Hong Kong's defence. The British were loath to arm these 'unreliable' men and lost the opportunity to increase their defence force with the volunteers. It was later suggested that about 75,000 of the 300,000 able-bodied Chinese men in Hong Kong would have fought in its defence if asked by the authorities.

The defence of Hong Kong island, which is 9 miles long by 3 miles wide, depended largely on its twenty-six coastal guns and fifty-six machine guns. These were installed in a number of forts and pillboxes which were manned by the Hong Kong and Singapore Artillery and units of Indian troops. There was also a handful of armoured cars crewed by a forty-man section, and these vehicles were locally made in Hong Kong workshops. In total the garrison had twenty-eight 'mobile' guns including a number of 2-pounder anti-tank guns.

Although the Hong Kong garrison had been expecting an invasion, the swiftness with which it followed the attack on Pearl Harbor took them by surprise. On the morning of 8 December Japanese planes bombed Hong Kong's Kai Tak airfield and destroyed the few RAF planes on its runway. This attack was quickly followed by the invasion from the north of the Leased Territories by the Imperial 38th Division. The 38th was a battle-hardened division under Lieutenant General Sano which quickly advanced to the colony's main defence line in the Leased Territories called the 'Gin Drinkers Line'.

General Maltby, the Commander in Chief in Hong Kong, had decided to change his plan to just defend Hong Kong island and abandon the Leased Territories to the Japanese. His new plan saw the reinforcement of the Gin Drinkers Line in the Leased Territories with three battalions and sixteen anti-tank and field guns. Heavy fighting took place along this defence line but the fall of its main redoubt at 'Shing Man' forced the defenders to retreat southwards. They withdrew on to Hong Kong island on the 14th and waited for the next attack by the forward units of the 38th Division. The small British garrison had had to be spread thinly in order to defend the island from all sides including the south. Here the coastal defences were threatened by the Imperial Navy and their attacks could only be countered by a few small defence boats and HMS *Cicala*, a poorly armed river gunboat. On the night of 18 December all three regiments of the 38th Division landed on the north shore of Hong Kong Island. In desperation the 'Loyal and Righteous' Chinese volunteers were offered a pistol and two grenades each on the

22nd but these were never delivered. On 25 December, just as the garrison was about to surrender, the volunteers were to be given twenty boxes of hand grenades and seventy-five machine guns. Meanwhile, the Japanese had advanced southwards across the island and soon reached the southern shore, splitting the island's defence in two. On Christmas Day the western sector of the British defence surrendered whilst the eastern sector resisted for one more day. The garrison was by then down to eight working guns and there was also a severe shortage of drinking water to contend with. The lack of water and supplies convinced General Maltby to give up the fight and ask for terms from the Japanese. Although the defenders had fought valiantly and had inflicted 2,754 casualties on the Japanese, they had lost 4,400 men in the 18-day battle for Hong Kong.

Indian troops dig trenches on the mainland to the north of Hong Kong in what were called the Leased Territories in the summer of 1941. The Leased Territories were originally leased from the Imperial Chinese government by the British in 1898 on a ninety-nine-year lease. When the Japanese occupied southern China from 1938 they begrudgingly honoured the agreement. Defending the Leased Territories was always going to be difficult with the limited troops at their disposal. One thought was that they shouldn't be defended at all whilst the garrison concentrated on defending the island itself and the port of Kowloon.

Canadian reinforcements arrive in Hong Kong just in time to take part in the brave but futile defence of the colony. The two battalions of Canadians were immediately pressed into front-line service and took up positions in the hills to the north of Hong Kong.

In effect theses soldiers were militia and had been designated as category 'C' which meant that they were unfit to serve overseas. They had received no training in the kind of fighting they were going to have to undertake during the coming battle. It was reported that most of the Canadians even had trouble distinguishing between the Chinese and Japanese. Their heavy equipment had been diverted to the Philippines apart from six Bren-gun carriers and they only had two Boys anti-tank rifles. In addition, they had no ammunition for the 2in and 3in trench mortars that they did have with them.

During the summer of 1941 the crew of a QF 2-pounder anti-tank gun of the Hong Kong garrison are going through their drill. The gun had a calibre of 40mm and was deemed to be too light to deal with German tanks in North Africa. It was still a useful weapon against Japanese light tanks but the defenders of Hong Kong had few artillery pieces of any type. According to the original quaint caption, the gun is 'tucked away on a hillside, ready for action'.

Soldiers of the Hong Kong Volunteer Defence Corps take part in pre-war training and are practising landing on one of the beaches on the mainland. The unit is made up of a few Europeans, in the foreground of the photograph, and Chinese volunteers in the background. The NCOs first out of the assault boat all appear to be armed with Thompson sub-machine guns whilst the other ranks have the standard Lee–Enfield .303s.

Soldiers of the Hong Kong Volunteer Defence Corps (HKVDC) parade outside the Southorn Stadium in the city in 1941. The HKVDC was made up of volunteers of various nationalities including two companies of neutral Portuguese. These troops were lightly armed and not particularly well trained but they gave a good account of themselves during the battle for the colony. In total there were 2,000 volunteers of the HKVDC involved in the defence of Hong Kong. Some regulars in the Hong Kong garrison derided the British volunteers as being wealthy 'playboy soldiers' but they fought as well as any of their comrades.

Chinese soldiers of the Hong Kong Fortress Company of Sappers parade in the centre of the city as war threatens. The Fortress Sappers was an engineer unit whose 800 or so troops fought as infantry in 1941. A last-minute intake of 150 recruits arrived too late to be trained and were sent to help man anti-aircraft guns during the battle for Hong Kong.

Two of the senior commanders in Hong Kong are seen here in conference on the eve of the Japanese attack. On the left is Major General C.M. Maltby, the General Officer in Command of the garrison. He is talking to Brigadier J.K. Lawson, the commander of the two Canadian units in Hong Kong. Brigadier Lawson was unfortunately to lose his life a few days later during the fighting for Hong Kong.

Two QF 3in 20 cwt anti-aircraft guns are put through their paces on the walls of Hong Kong harbour in 1941. This outdated gun had been the mainstay of the anti-aircraft defences of the British Empire from 1914. By the Second World War it had been replaced by the 3.7in gun in British army service but there were many still in service in the colonies.

The Indian crew of a 3in anti-aircraft gun man their gun near hills in the Leased Territories. At first it was intended only to defend Hong Kong Island itself but then General Maltby decided to move his defence line to the mainland. It didn't really matter what defence plan Maltby enacted because Hong Kong was doomed from the moment that Japan went to war with the British Empire.

Japanese medium artillery fire from the hills around Hong Kong onto the British defences. The assault was launched at 07.30 am on 8 December, only 4 hours after the attack on Pearl Harbor. In total the Japanese had 20,000 men organized in 9 infantry battalions and 17 artillery battalions. They were supported by 6 air squadrons and a small Imperial naval force which immediately imposed a blockade of Hong Kong port. In the first hours the defenders blew up a vital bridge over the Shan Chun River which was soon repaired by Japanese engineers. At the same time the Japanese destroyed all five British planes at Hong Kong's Kai Tak airport, although these were all non-combat aircraft.

Chinese guerrillas operating in Kwangtung province close to Hong Kong in December 1941. They were supposed to be relieving the pressure on the colony. Chiang Kai-shek had ordered a relief column of Nationalist troops to move towards Hong Kong but this did not happen. Hong Kong had been isolated since the late 1930s and the events of 7 December sealed its fate.

The British navy river gunboat Insect class HMS *Cicala*, launched in 1915, sails through Hong Kong harbour where she was to support the defence of the colony in December 1941. She was armed with two 6in guns and a 2-pounder pom-pom anti-aircraft gun as well as eight Lewis light machine guns. Described by her captain Lieutenant Commander John Bolero as a 'one armed dugout', the *Cicala's* fifty-seven-strong crew struggled manfully to keep her in action throughout the fighting. After enduring a total of twenty-three air attacks and still managing to stay in action she was finally dive-bombed on 20 December and had to be abandoned by her crew.

Japanese troops rush through the port area of Hong Kong as the city is falling on Christmas Day, 1941. In two days the Japanese had advanced 15 miles across the mainland and on the second night took the important Shin Mun Redoubt. This was a heavily defended position protected by barbed wire and five pillboxes with interconnecting tunnels. The redoubt was manned by the 2nd Battalion Royal Scots Regiment which on losing control of it tried to retake it. However, too many of the battalion's men were ill with malaria and the counter-attack failed.

British, Canadian and Indian troops march into captivity after the fall of Hong Kong. They were to spend the next four years in brutal conditions. When Hong Kong fell the Japanese army ran amok committing the same kind of mindless atrocities that they had in Nanking and other Chinese cities. They killed the wounded in hospitals and mass raped the nurses who had been caring for them. Groups of Canadian and British prisoners were bayoneted and any Chinese who had fought in the defence of Hong Kong could expect little mercy.

The Japanese commander at Hong Kong, Lieutenant General Takashi Sakai, rides into the city at the head of his officers as his troops salute him. Whilst this parade was taking place there were a large number of massacres of surrendering soldiers being carried out by Imperial troops. In addition, many medical staff, civil defence workers and civilian volunteers were also executed after surrendering. These killings may not have been officially sanctioned but the high-ranking Japanese officers turned a blind eye to them anyway.

Chapter Seven

The Malayan Campaign, 1941-2

The British possessions in Malaya had always been the initial target for the Japanese land offensives in South-East Asia. Japanese plans for the conquest of Malaya had been long in the making, and an attack on the British naval base on Singapore island on its southern tip had first been muted in 1931. Besides the large naval base, the Japanese were also interested in the rubber and tin produced in Malaya. The country accounted for 38 per cent of the world's rubber and 58 per cent of the world's tin production, and for a natural resources-starved country such as Japan this made Malaya a tempting target. The country depended largely on imports of rice to feed its 5 million people as much of the country was covered in jungle and plantations. The impenetrable jungle of central Malaya was seen as the best protection that Singapore could have. Unfortunately for the British, the Japanese had other ideas about the difficulty of advancing through jungle and had been training their troops for this eventuality.

The Japanese invasion fleet for Malaya was spotted in the Gulf of Siam on 6 December but no action was to be taken by the British until war officially broke out. On 8 December Japanese landings took place at Kota Bharu on the north-eastern coast of Malaya and here 5,500 troops came ashore. At the same time two separate landings were taking place at the two Thai ports of Singora and Patani. In response the British sent their two capital ships from Singapore, HMS *Prince of Wales* and HMS *Repulse*, northwards but both were sunk by Japanese aircraft on the 10th (see Chapter Twelve). This naval defeat was a major blow to Allied morale but the war was to be won on land not at sea. In total 110,000 Japanese soldiers eventually came ashore in Malaya or crossed the Thai–Malayan border, although only 70,000 of these were combat troops. They were to be faced by 88,600 Allied soldiers made up of British, Australian and Indian troops under the command of the uninspiring General Percival. During the campaign further Allied reinforcements were landed at Singapore but numbers did not seem to count in this one-sided campaign.

In the west of Malaya the British positions at Alor Star fell on the 12th. Here the Japanese took the airfield with the runway undamaged as well as stock of bombs and fuel. Four days later the island of Penang off the western coast fell to the advancing

Japanese army. On 13 December the Japanese also attacked vital Allied defences at Jitra in the north-west which were held by Indian troops. The Imperial Army's advance got properly underway.

Late December saw the landings behind Allied lines of Japanese forces on the east coast of Malaya at Kuala Trengganu, Kuala Bungun and Kuantan. This tactic by the Imperial Army allowed a almost uncontested advance to the Johore defence line, which was the last chance for the demoralized Allied forces. On the western side of Malaya a series of desperate defensive positions fell at Ipoh on 28 December and two further positions north of Kuala Lumpur, the capital. Kuala Lumpur duly fell on 11 January and the Japanese continued to advance southwards towards Johore State.

Japanese offensive tactics during the Malayan Campaign were nearly always successful with one of the most effective being the allocation of one-third of an attacking force to the frontal assault. The other two-thirds were then given the task of outflanking the defenders and attacking them from the side or their rear. The morale of Allied troops during the withdrawal through Malaya was at a low ebb as they constantly retreated, dug in and then retreated again only to dig in further south. At the same time the Japanese used their air superiority to bomb and strafe them further affecting their fighting spirit. As one commentator said, they were soon fighting on the edge of despair and 'acting like automatons'.

By early January the British forces were totally exhausted after three weeks of continuous fighting which had ended invariably in a series of defeats. A desperate battle took place at the Slim River on 7 January and resulted in another disaster for the Allied Army when 3,200 British troops surrendered to the Japanese. The 11th Indian Division was totally destroyed in this battle and many Allied units now tried to reorganize under constant pressure from the Japanese. Central Malaya was lost after the defeat at Slim River and the only course of action appeared to be to withdraw to the south and prepare some kind of southern bastion. General Wavell, the overall commander of the Allied forces in South-East Asia, now ordered General Percival to withdraw his remaining forces to Johore State in the far south. This part of the Malayan peninsula was narrower and it was hoped that if the Allied troops could establish a defensive line there it might be possible to hold it. By 15 January the majority of the Allied troops had managed to reach this new defensive line, but most were now totally demoralized. They had little time to prepare themselves before the Japanese began penetrating the line's defences on the 17th.

A Japanese defeat at Gemas on 18 January was one of the few positives of the campaign but this did not stop the Imperial Army's advance. The usual fear of being outflanked and surrounded now led to some units abandoning their positions. Further retreats followed and the majority of the Allied Army continued to retreat further south until they reached the coast opposite Singapore on the 31st. During the retreat there were a number of brave rearguard actions by Allied troops who had managed to maintain some morale. Percival now issued orders for the withdrawal of his remaining forces on to Singapore island.

In this rather grainy Japanese official photograph Imperial Army troops come ashore in northern Malaya from wooden landing boats. At 00.45 am on 8 December, 70 minutes before the strike on Pearl Harbor, 5,500 Japanese troops landed off the northern Malayan port of Kota Bharu. A few hours later further landings were made at Singora and Patani in southern Thailand and these troops moved swiftly to the Thai–Malayan border. At the same time the Imperial Guards Division was moving from French Indo-China through Thai territory in preparation to join the campaign to conquer Malaya.

A 3in mortar crew of the 2/9th Gurkha Regiment in the Malayan jungle are put through their paces in the weeks leading up to outbreak of hostilities with Japan. The photograph is posed purely for the news cameraman as can be seen by the fact that the mortar still has its cover on. Five battalions of Gurkhas fought in the defence of Malaya with the 2/1st being one of the first units to encounter the Japanese. This unit was overrun by Japanese tanks on 10 December and as a result lost three-quarters of its men.

In this highly symbolic photograph a platoon of Japanese troops charge on to a RAF airfield in the north of Malaya and clamber over the wing of a wrecked British transport plane. The Japanese overrunning of the northern Malayan air bases ruined the British Eastern Command's air based defence plan for Malaya and Singapore. Some of the RAF bases had been recently constructed in western Malaya to accommodate an expected 566 modern aircraft. When the war with Japan broke out there were only 158 first-line aircraft in Malaya along with a number of transports, liaison planes and training aircraft.

A column of determined looking Imperial Army troops march across a Malayan river in the first days of the invasion. Landings had been made by the 25th Imperial Army at several points in northern Malaya on 8 December with the 5th Division landing on the coast of Thailand. At the same time the 18th Division came ashore at Kota Bharu on Malaya's north-east coast. The Indian troops who defended the north were either beaten in battle or bypassed as the Japanese advanced swiftly southwards.

The 3rd Air Group of the Netherlands East Indies Army Air Corps arrives in Singapore in December 1941. Its personnel are being greeted by Air Chief Marshal Sir Robert Brooke-Popham, the Commander in Chief of the British Far East Command. As part of the mutual defence arrangements between the Dutch and the British the former promised to send five squadrons to assist in the defence of Malaya.

A tough-looking soldier of the Malay Regiment looks defiantly into the camera with his trusty Lee–Enfield rifle slung over his shoulder. The first Malayan unit, an experimental company, had been established in 1933 with a strength of 800 men. In 1935 this unit was re-named the Malay Regiment and plans were made for another battalion of 450 to be added to it. Malay Regiment units were deployed throughout the peninsula from early December.

This 3in mortar crew of the Malay Regiment is training with its weapon in the jungle in late 1941. By the time the regiment had been withdrawn to Singapore it had reached a strength of 1,400 men. Some reinforcements had been seconded from the Malay element of the Straits Settlement Volunteer Force. During the fighting in Malaya and Singapore units of the Malay Regiment made a series of last-ditch stands against the advancing Japanese.

A commander of a Lanchester armoured car signals to other vehicles of his unit in a training exercise before the war. The Lanchester Mk I, M1927 armoured car was an outdated and heavy design which was poorly armed with three Vickers machine guns. There was a .50 and .303 machine gun in the turret and a .303 in the hull alongside the driver. The Lanchesters in Malaya were handed over to the Argyll and Sutherland Highlanders whose infantrymen were given a crash training course to operate them.

An Australian artillery forward radio operator lies in a slit trench in the north of Malaya relaying information back to his battery. The main fear of all Allied troops in the Malayan campaign was being outflanked by the Japanese. Imperial Army jungle training included crawling silently towards enemy positions covered in camouflage. Although most simply attached foliage to their belts and helmets, others wore specially made camouflage suits. These were worn particularly by snipers who were trained to wait in trees and pick off officers as they passed underneath.

British and Australian troops work together carrying a wooden walkway into position during an exercise in December 1941. As sometimes happened during the First World War, there was often an uneasy relationship between the two allies especially in the higher ranks. The Australian government had committed large numbers of troops to the North African theatre and the 8th Division to Malaya. This left only 1 Brigade of the 8th to defend Australia if the war went badly for the Allies. Despite pleas from the British High Command, the Australians refused to send troops to Burma in 1942 saying they had to think of the defence of their country.

Japanese troops cross one of the small rivers and creeks in Malaya using a simple bridge made from a few tree trunks. Their engineer comrades form human supports whilst they get across before assessing if they need to build a more permanent structure. The Imperial Army emphasized the importance of keeping their troops moving forward by having a full regiment of engineers on the strength of each infantry division. One Japanese officer boasting about his troops' performance in Malaya said, 'On an average our troops had fought two battles, repaired four or five bridges and had advanced 20 kilometres per day'.

Australian troops have confiscated a native wooden boat and mounted a light deck gun from a British ship on the foredeck. It was to be used to patrol some of the rivers, mangrove swamps and creeks of the Malayan peninsula. Malaya, like most South-East Asian countries, had a large number of creeks and small rivers. These along with the jungle were thought by the British to be a major obstacle to the Japanese advance down the peninsula.

Japanese troops sheltering behind a Type 94 light tank move into the centre of Kuala Lumpar on 11 January. When the city fell the Japanese captured much-needed stores including a lot of food stuffs. Most of the petrol supplies had, however, been destroyed and some equipment had been sent southwards on the orders of the Allied Command. One particularly important capture in Kuala Lumpar was a stash of detailed maps of the British defences of Singapore.

Imperial Army troops rush across open ground in the centre of Kuala Lumpar on 11 January as a supply dump burns in the background. The Malayan capital was not defended as the Allied troops retreated further south towards the 'sanctuary' of Singapore. When the Japanese took the city they captured huge stores of food, arms and clothing and many motor vehicles. Although orders had gone out to set fire to all the fuel dumps, some did not burn and were captured intact by the Imperial Army.

The Japanese victory in Malaya was not won without loss as this dead pilot shot down by anti-aircraft fire personifies. British, Australian and Indian anti-aircraft gun crews were well trained and outfought some Japanese bombers and fighters. Their success rate was helped by the gung-ho tactics of the Japanese pilots who flew low over Allied positions.

A lone British or Australian soldier is searched after been captured in the fighting in the north of Malaya. His fate depends on the whim of the Japanese officer in command as the Geneva Convention was not able to protect him. Some prisoners were treated humanely whilst others according to eyewitnesses were swiftly bayoneted or beheaded. The 5th Imperial Division troops serving in Malaya were mostly veterans of the Battle of Shanghai in 1937. The troops had become hardened to war during their service in China where prisoners were never taken.

During the Malayan Campaign 2 squadrons of Netherlands East Indies Martin 139 WH-1 bombers were sent to help the British. They were stationed at Singapore and performed a number of reconnaissance missions during December 1941 but were not allowed to bomb the enemy. Belonging to the 1 and 2 VLG III units, about fifteen of these planes were eventually given permission to take part in bombing raids alongside British Blenheim and Australian Hudson bombers. They also fought with Royal Australian Air Force Brewster Buffalo fighters before being evacuated to Java where they participated in their last battles.

This Japanese pre-production Nakajima KI-44 was flown by Captain Yashiko Kuroe during the 1941–2 fighting. His first recorded kill was in January 1942 when he was facing the inferior fighters and bombers of the Allied forces. The KI-44 was the latest type in service in 1941–2 and was tested in battle before full production began. Although not popular with pilots initially because of its heavy handling, its victories over Malaya meant it was accepted into full service.

Japanese troops attacking a town on the island of Penang off the west coast of Malaya. They have temporarily discarded their bicycles whilst they follow their officer into the attack. When the main garrison of the island was withdrawn the only defenders left were the poorly armed 850 men of the 'Penang & Province Wellesley Volunteer Corps'. They stayed to defend their home island from the Kobayashi Battalion whose 1,000 men landed in stages from 17–19 December.

Indian troops of an unidentified unit are patiently waiting at a port in Malaya to be sent to the front line. They may belong to the 45th Infantry Brigade which had been formed in 1941 and trained for desert warfare. Instead, they were sent to Singapore where they arrived on 3 January and were sent immediately to the front line. By 10 January they were down to 1,000 men having fought hard against the Imperial Guards Division. Their commander was killed on 20 January and the battered survivors were disbanded on 1 February 1942.

The ground crew of a Mitsubishi G3M long-range bomber service the engine of their plane before an operation over Malaya. This type of bomber had been responsible for the sinking of the British navy's capital ships, HMS *Prince of Wales* and HMS *Repulse,* on 10 December 1941. First delivered to the Japanese Imperial Air Force in 1936, its long range was the reason it was chosen to attack the two battleships. The captains of the ships had thought that they were too far out to sea to be hit by a land-based bomber.

Well-camouflaged Japanese troops move down a small river during their advance through the Malayan peninsula. The best Imperial Army troops were highly trained especially in night fighting which put the Allied soldiers at a great disadvantage. They were trained to recognize jungle noises and distinguish them from sounds of the enemy moving about. In comparison, they were trained to move about in silence and to crawl up to enemy positions. A special crawling technique was taught to recruits which involved cradling their rifle in both arms as they moved forward.

This cover of a Japanese pictorial magazine of 1942 shows an Imperial Army propaganda unit calling for the surrender of enemy troops by loud speaker. The Japanese were experts at using such tactics, especially against the native troops of the British, US and Dutch armies. As defeat followed defeat in Malaya this method was employed alongside the use of turncoat captured soldiers and volunteers. These would approach the trenches held by Indian troops and call for them to join the Japanese in liberating Asia from the colonial powers.

A long column of Type 95 light tanks covered in foliage for camouflage moves down a Malayan road. This kind of formation was susceptible to attack from the thick jungle on either side of the road. Some Japanese tankers were to pay for their arrogance in assuming that the Allied troops would not attack from the available cover. The Type 95 was armed with a 37mm main gun which was operated by the tank commander alone. As the French had found out in 1940, the commander having to fire the main armament was a great disadvantage in tank-on-tank battles.

The Japanese were noted for their ability to adapt to the conditions they faced in Malaya and the use of bicycles in large numbers supports this belief. Described by some as the Japanese 'secret weapon', the humble bicycle certainly gave mobility to some Imperial Army troops. It could be used on the roads and carried through the jungle when necessary. These troops are pushing theirs along and carrying all their equipment on the frame or handlebars. One of the main problems in using bicycles in the heat of Malaya was the number of punctures sustained.

A Japanese light artillery unit moves along a Malayan road carrying their guns broken down on the backs of their mules. The guns are 75mm Type 41s which could be broken down into six parts but could also easily be towed. It was an adaptation of an earlier gun produced from 1908 and given a lighter carriage in the 1930s. Before modification it was described as a mountain gun but after 1934 was re-designated a regimental gun.

This photograph taken from a wartime Japanese propaganda magazine shows an infantry unit of the Imperial Army at Gemas in southern Malaya on 14 January 1942. The soldiers are moving stealthily through the undergrowth up a slope in the approaches to the city which fell on the 15th. One great myth of the Far East Campaign was that the average Imperial Army soldier was 'at home' in the jungle. In reality most Japanese, even though from rural backgrounds, had never seen jungle of the type encountered in Malaya.

During their advance southwards through Malaya the Japanese Imperial Army suffered few setbacks. A rare success for the Allied Army saw this unit of Type 95 tanks ambushed and destroyed by the 13th Battery of the 4th Australian Anti-tank Regiment. The Japanese tankers were halted in their tracks by felled trees which lay across the paved road near Gemas close to the Maur River on 18 January.

Another view of the ambush shows dead Japanese soldiers laid at the side of their destroyed Type 95 'Ha-go' light tanks. Nine or ten Japanese tanks were destroyed in this fierce engagement by two 2-pounder anti-tank guns. Japanese infantry also suffered heavy losses during the fighting around Gemas, and up to 1,000 were reported killed. Although this action was a major setback for the Imperial Army, it did not affect their unstoppable advance towards Singapore. This rare victory for the Allies was, however, featured in various publications and news spread throughout the Allied ranks. It certainly helped to raise the morale temporarily of the Australian and British troops who were weary of retreating day after day.

One of the Australian anti-tank gun crews that destroyed the Japanese tanks is seen looking down the sights of their 2-pounder gun. The lightweight gun could penetrate 53mm of armour at a range of 500yd whilst the Type 95 had a maximum of 12mm armour thickness. Once the tanks had been halted by the road block they were sitting targets for the well-trained Australians.

An Australian soldier aims from behind the cover of a rubber tree during a skirmish with the Japanese in January 1942. With their limited resources stretched fighting in North Africa and South-East Asia, the quality of some of the 1,900 reinforcements who arrived in Malaya in late January was questionable. One British commander went as far as to say that some of the Australians who had been sent to fight were really the 'sweepings of jails'. This kind of comment did not go down well with the Australian commanders who were, however, aware of the shortcomings of some of the new arrivals.

A Japanese army officer rests during the advance through Malaya and cools himself with a rising sun emblazoned fan. It was probably brought with him from his home and would have been presented to him by his proud family. Most Imperial Army soldiers had sashes and other keepsakes with good luck messages from their families back home. The 'belt of a thousand stitches' with messages sewn onto it was a particularly poignant item for the Japanese soldier to take to the battlefront.

The artillery crew of a Japanese 75mm Type 91 light field gun fires towards Allied lines in Malaya having stripped to the waist in the heat. This gun was one of the most modern in Japanese service in 1941 and had been copied from the French Schneider 1927. It entered service in 1930 and was modernized during the 1930s and had pneumatic tyres fitted to replace the original wooden ones. Two of the crew are wearing the second model of the Imperial Army cork sun helmet along with tropical uniform trousers.

Chapter Eight

'The British Army's Greatest Defeat' – The Fall of Singapore, 1942

The unstoppable advance of the Japanese Imperial Army down the Malayan peninsula between early December and late January ended with the taking of Johore State. Although some Allied units continued to fight, they were now bravely covering the retreat of their comrades on to the island of Singapore, off the southern tip of Malaya. The naval base on Singapore Island had always been the main target for the Japanese invasion. Since the 1930s Singapore's defences had been centred at the naval base in the south of the island. Unfortunately, the ships that were projected to defend the base and island had not been provided by the British government due to budget cuts in the late 1930s. An alternative defence plan for Malaya and Singapore depended on the presence of 566 modern aircraft, but in 1941–2 there were only 158, and many of these were obsolete. Responsibility for defence would now be left to the garrison of the island, reinforced by thousands of demoralized troops who had repeatedly been defeated by the Japanese in Malaya. These defeated British forces had withdrawn across the causeway between Malaya and Singapore between 29 and 31 January. Once the last troops were across, the causeway was blown up and the 80,000 British, Indian, Australian and Malayan volunteers prepared to defend this last enclave of British power in the region. On 31 January Lieutenant General Percival issued a message about the situation in Malaya. It said: 'The battle of Malaya has come to an end and the battle of Singapore has started'.

Winston Churchill said he was astounded by how weak Singapore's landward defences were and how no commander had seen fit to reinforce them during 1941. Even though it was probable that Singapore would have to be defended, no real defence measures were taken from December 1941 until February 1942.

The Japanese army that now threatened Singapore was at the end of its tether, the troops totally exhausted and ammunition stocks low. Even if the British had realized how weak the Japanese were, there was little fight left in many of the defenders. The Japanese commander, General Yamashita, summed up the situation when he later said:

My attack on Singapore was a bluff, a bluff that worked. I had 30,000 men and was outnumbered by more than three to one. I knew that if I had to fight long for Singapore I would be beaten, that's why the surrender had to be at once. I was very frightened that all the time that the British would discover our numerical weakness and lack of supplies and force me into disastrous street fighting.

On the night of 8–9 February the first Japanese troops crossed the straits from Johore on to Singapore Island. They landed on the north-west coast of the island, which was defended by 5 Australian battalions, and by dawn there were 13,000 troops ashore. Isolated Allied units defended their own positions so that there was no co-ordinated defence. These pockets of resistance, with little communication between them, were each in turn outflanked and overwhelmed by the Japanese. By the 10th nearly all the available 30,000 Japanese were on Singapore and in most sectors the Allied troops were having to withdraw under pressure. Several brave counter-attacks by the defenders failed and they fell back towards Singapore City. Japanese tanks had been landed on the island and the air force flew a series of devastating raids on the city, which was crowded with refugees. On the 15th the Japanese captured the main water supply plant and the fate of Singapore was now sealed. With hundreds of thousands of civilians suffering and an estimated 7,000 of them having been killed in the Japanese air raids, Percival had to make a difficult decision. He was also now confronted by officers who came from their hard-pressed units to tell him that further resistance was futile. After discussions with his commanders, he offered a conditional surrender to the Japanese on the evening of the 15th. This was rejected face to face by Yamashita, who thought that the British might realize how precarious the position of his forces was. Percival was quickly pressured into accepting the unconditional surrender and duly signed the agreement. A greatly relieved Yamashita now took the unconditional surrender of the garrison and completed a great victory against all the odds. The exhausted and humiliated Allied troops waited patiently to be led into an unexpectedly cruel captivity. As the soldiers were marched away to holding camps they did not know that they were to face years of brutal treatment, disease and starvation at the hands of the Japanese.

At the end of the fighting in Malaya and Singapore the Allies had lost 9,000 killed and wounded and 130,000 British, Indian and Australian troops had been taken into captivity. The Japanese had also suffered heavy casualties with 3,000 killed and over 6,000 wounded. The scale of the defeat of the British forces was a shock to those who were not in the Far East but not to those familiar with the situation on the ground. General Wavell commented on hearing about the fall of Singapore, 'The trouble goes back a long way: the climate, the atmosphere of the country, lack of vigour in our peacetime training, and the cumbrousness of our tactics and equipment, and the real difficulty in finding an answer to the very skilful and bold tactics of the Japanese in the jungle fighting'.

Lieutenant General A.E. Percival, DSO,OBE, the General Officer in Command in Malaya, is usually made the scapegoat for the British defeat in 1941–2. Percival did make some strategic mistakes during the campaign, and he was not rated by either his superior Wavell or the Australian commander General Pownall. Wavell undermined Percival at the height of the fighting by intervening in his plans whilst still leaving him in command. It would have taken a better commander than Percival to save the situation but Wavell's interference did not bring any improvement to the dire circumstances. The poor training and general unpreparedness of most of the Allied troops and the unexpected performance of the Japanese Imperial Army meant the end result was inevitable.

Soldiers of the 5th Sikh Regiment disembark in Singapore as reinforcements for the struggling Allied Force in Malaya. During the Malayan Campaign an additional 15,000 Indian soldiers arrived to bolster the 88,600 troops already in the region. They were joined by 19,000 British and 3,000 Australian reinforcements which brought the Allied strength up to 125,000 men. Indian units in Malaya were made up of men from various ethnic and religious groups including Sikhs, Dogras, Baluchs, Jats and Punjabis. They were kept in separate regiments to avoid any inter-religious or regional rivalries spilling over into hostilities.

One of the big guns defending Singapore is seen in its concrete emplacement with a camouflage screen over it. Although it is not true to say that all the big guns of the fortress were 'pointing the wrong way', some were badly positioned to defend the landward direction. In reality when the Japanese attack began two-thirds of the guns of Singapore were able to turn around to shell them. Many of the guns had been positioned to defend the strategic Keppel Harbour and the naval base, which cost £63,000,000. The majority of guns were on the eastern tip of the island or down in the south. Only the Pasir Laba Battery, which had two 6in guns, was actually facing the Malay peninsula directly.

This concrete gun emplacement in the Singapore defences is manned by Indian fortress artillerymen. The turret of the gun is painted in a camouflage pattern and a frame over it supports netting to help disguise it from air attack. In reality the Japanese knew the position of every gun emplacement before they began their attack on Singapore. They had gained this information over the years from a highly effective network of agents. Agents had been working in South-East Asia as shopkeepers, merchants and other tradesmen including photographers. If more information on the defences of Singapore was required the detailed plans captured during the Malayan Campaign certainly provided it.

Soldiers of the Malay Regiment move at the double across open ground in pre-war training exercises. Two brigades of Malay troops were part of the garrison of Singapore in 1942 and were described as being of 'low quality, poorly trained and indifferently led'. When the fighting began some Malayans fought well when led by officers they respected despite their lack of training. One unit under the command of Lieutenant Adnan Saidi fought to last man in its position at Pasir Panjang in Singapore.

Indian heavy artillerymen on Singapore train with their 6in 26 cwt howitzer, which first saw service in 1915. Most of these out-of-date heavy guns were upgraded in the 1930s with the addition of pneumatic tyres and brake mechanisms. The majority of these guns were lost with the British Expeditionary Force in France in 1940 and the survivors fought in the Western Desert in 1940–1. This gun still has the old metal wheels fitted and probably has not been modified in any way since its First World War service.

Two Marmon-Herrington Mk III armoured cars of the 3rd Indian Cavalry Regiment move through the streets of Singapore City. These armoured cars arrived in Singapore from their previous service in the North African desert in a parlous state. Worn out, poorly maintained and often lacking some of their equipment, they even had desert sand in their cabs. Many arrived with no armament and the most they could expect was a Vickers machine gun hastily fitted in the turret.

Wounded soldiers are brought into a Singapore hospital from the battles that were raging over most of the island. The ambulance drivers were often Chinese volunteers who also served in most other civil defence organizations. Many were to be badly treated by the Japanese when they took Singapore because they had supported the British. Others were arrested and often killed simply for being Chinese and being seen by the Japanese as supporters of Chiang Kai-shek and his Nationalist government.

Singapore firemen try to tackle a blaze in the centre of the city as the noose tightens around the island. As the Japanese moved southwards down the Malayan peninsula their bombers softened up Singapore with increasing air raids. The civil defenders of Singapore were largely made up of members of the Chinese community. Chinese communities all over the Far East had supported either Chiang Kai-shek or the Chinese Communist Party. The British authorities were cautious at first about arming potential Communist sympathizers. This attitude changed eventually but far too late to affect the outcome of the fighting in Singapore.

Sobbing Chinese women lament the deaths of their loved ones after a bombing raid by the Japanese on Singapore. The peacetime population of Singapore had been swelled by 500,000 refugees escaping from the fighting on the mainland. Conditions for the civilian population were bad enough but the bombing of the over-crowded island by the Japanese made the situation unbearable. When General Percival was considering whether to surrender the island to the Japanese the situation of the civilian population had to be taken into account.

In this poor quality action photograph the Indian crew of a British-made 3in 20 cwt anti-aircraft gun is seen firing the gun at Japanese bombers attacking Singapore. According to the caption, this image was taken in the last few days before the fall of Singapore when some of the heaviest air attacks on Singapore City took place. As the Japanese troops who had landed in the north-west of the island advanced their air force softened up the already demoralized troops and civilians on the rest of the island.

Japanese troops prepare to cross the repaired causeway from Johore Bahru to Singapore and are gathered around their Type 94 light tanks. The 30,000 Japanese troops were outnumbered by the Allied garrison but their morale was sky high. In contrast, the British, Australian, Indian and Malayan troops who made up the Singapore garrison were totally demoralized. When the Japanese landed on Singapore Island the Allied troops put up a good fight but it was only a matter of time before they were defeated.

Chinese volunteers of Dalleyforce, or 'Dalforce' as it was usually known, parade in front of their headquarters in Singapore. This last-ditch defence force was also known as the 'Singapore Overseas Chinese Anti-Japanese Volunteer Army'. It was recruited from members of the Chinese Communist Party and the Kuomintang Party and had a strength of 4,000 by the time the Japanese invaded. Commanded by Lieutenant Colonel John Dalley of the Federated Malay Police, it was poorly armed with Lee–Enfields and a few sporting guns and small calibre 'bird guns'. Bullets for the Lee–Enfields were shared out according to the political affiliation of the volunteer with Communists getting 7–20 and the Kuomintang getting 24! There was no uniform only an armband with Dalforce stamped on it and a red cloth tied around the right arm and a yellow scarf wrapped around their heads.

These young men are from another of the volunteer units raised from the Chinese population of Singapore in 1941–2. They belong to the 'Overseas Chinese Guard Force' which was raised from amongst the Kuomintang-supporting population. It was part of Dalforce and was trained by British officers in the weeks before the Japanese attack on Singapore. The front row of volunteers are armed with Lee–Enfield .303s whilst the men in the back row appear to be armed with sporting guns.

When the fall of Singapore was inevitable an order was issued by the command to destroy any equipment and weaponry that might be of use to the Japanese. These men are obeying that instruction by lining up army staff cars on the harbour walls and pushing them into the sea. Although a lot of British equipment was destroyed, the Japanese managed to capture plenty of Bren-gun carriers, armoured cars and artillery pieces. Some of these were later handed over to the newly formed pro-Japanese Indian National Army. In total 740 artillery pieces, 200 armoured cars, 65,000 small arms and 2,500 machine guns were lost during the Malayan Campaign.

General Percival and his staff officers walk to their surrender meeting with the Japanese commanding officer, General Yamashita, in Singapore on the evening of 15 February. Yamashita knew he had to force the British commander to surrender immediately in order to stop Percival realizing how weak the Imperial Army was. Both commanders were in reality in poor positions and the Japanese had used the last of their ammunition during the fighting. Percival had to worry about the large numbers of civilians under his care with little water available and knew that most of his soldiers had had enough.

In this propaganda photograph of the fall of Singapore, Allied and Japanese troops fraternize and share cigarettes. This may have been a genuine friendly encounter between the victorious Japanese and these British or Australian soldiers. The Japanese soldiers total lack of respect for anyone who surrendered meant that scenes like this would have been a rarity. Even if a Japanese soldier was inclined to treat his foes with humanity, he was under pressure from his officers and comrades to be brutal to them. Japanese soldiers were totally indifferent to the fate of their prisoners and neglected them terribly, which led to the deaths of thousands of prisoners of war due to shortages of food and water.

British and Australian troops are marched to their captivity in holding camps on Singapore Island whilst their Japanese captors mill around in the background. One man smiles nervously at the Japanese photographers whilst his comrades look demoralized and concerned about what the future might hold. None of them had any idea what privations they were to suffer during three years of captivity until the survivors were liberated in August 1945. The Japanese could not comprehend why so many men had allowed themselves to be captured in February 1942. They regarded all Allied prisoners of war as an insignificant inconvenience who were unworthy of their consideration.

Chapter Nine

Battle for the Philippines, 1941-2

T he Japanese plan for the conquest of South-East Asia and the setting up of a 'Greater East Asian Co-Prosperity Sphere' included the Philippines. Although the Philippines Commonwealth had been given a type of semi-independence, until full independence in 1944 the USA still had a strong military presence there. Japan's plans for the invasion of the Philippines would be put into action as soon as the attack on Pearl Harbor had taken place.

In December 1941 the defence of the Philippines was divided into three sectors with the main island of Luzon divided into the North Luzon Force and South Luzon Force. Anywhere south of Luzon came under the Visayan-Mindanao Force, which covered Visayan and Mindanao as well as Samar, Leyte, Panay, Mindoro, Negros and Cebu. The North Luzon Force had 4 infantry divisions and 1 cavalry regiment, the South Luzon Force had 2 divisions and the Visayan-Mindanao Force had 3 divisions with a 2-division reserve force in the vicinity of Manila. The air defence of the Philippines was in the hands of the American Far East Air Force (AFEAF), which was seen by the Japanese as a major threat to their plans. It was a 227-plane-strong force with 100 modern fighters and 35 heavy B-17 bombers on strength. The AFEA was stationed mainly at Clark Field, which was dangerously within range of the Japanese Air Force. On 8 December at 12.35 pm the first Japanese air raids took place on the US air force bases at Clark Field and El Carmen airfield on the island of Luzon. These raids by fifty-three Japanese bombers were protected by the famed Zero fighters which destroyed any US P-40 or P-35 fighters that managed to get airborne. After the bombers had done their work destroying so many of the US fighters and B-17 bombers on the ground, the Zeros took over. Some strafed any planes on the ground that had escaped the bombing raids whilst their comrades knocked any US fighters out of the sky in an unequal battle. The US losses totalled 17 B-17 bombers, 56 fighters of various types and 30 liaison and transport planes. After 11 hours of raids the US air force in the Philippines was virtually destroyed and the ground invasion could begin without interference.

The first landings by the Imperial Army's 14th Army took place in the north of Luzon, troops coming ashore at the ports of Aparri and Vigan on 10 December. Two battalions were landed there to capture the US air bases which could then be used as forward bases by the Japanese Imperial Air Force. These first landings were followed two days later by Japanese landings in south-eastern Luzon. On 22 December the Japanese landed the main invasion force in western Luzon in the Lingayen Gulf. The 43,100 men of 14th Army were landed from 84 transport ships in bad weather but were soon established on the island. They were faced by thousands of poorly trained Filipino troops who were soon scattered by the advancing Japanese.

Imperial Army units now headed south-eastwards towards Manila. Other units moved south-westwards to destroy any Filipino divisions in the region to secure their army's rear. General Wainwright, the US commander of the North Luzon Force, sent some of his best units to try and hold the line just as the Japanese arrived. Now the same Filipino units that had retreated in front of the Japanese fought hard to hold off the Imperial Army. During this period many Filipinos received the kind of training which had been lacking at the start of the campaign. Now that they were mixed in with US and better Filipino troops, such as the Philippines Scouts, they invariably fought well. While the Filipino and US troops were fighting desperately to hold back the Japanese, defences were being prepared on the Bataan peninsula. Bataan, on the south-western point of Luzon, was a large peninsula that jutted out into Manila Bay, the prized deep-water harbour that the Japanese coveted. In late December, Filipino-US forces had begun to be withdrawn from the rest of Luzon into Bataan. In January, 80,000 troops and 36,000 civilians were waiting for the Japanese to finish mopping up the rest of the Filipino positions before attacking Bataan. The Northern Defence Line, defended by three divisions, was struck by the Japanese on 9 January, but held out against them for several weeks. On 26 January, the Filipino-US forces were withdrawn southwards down the peninsula to a new defence line about half-way down Bataan. After a few assaults against the Southern Defence Line, there followed a lull as both sides rested and the Japanese brought in more reinforcements. The defenders of Bataan were suffering from hunger and disease, and a lack of mosquito nets resulted in a large number of cases of malaria. Filipino soldiers now used their skills to hunt for game, including buffalo, snakes, wild pigs and chickens, to supplement their diet and shared their bounty with their US comrades. Shortages of staple foods and cigarettes nevertheless affected the troops' morale and rations had to be cut.

On 3 April, the much-reinforced Japanese attacked the Southern Defence Line and the defenders' spirits were finally broken. The southern defences were manned by 60,000 men, but they were exhausted, hungry and frequently suffering from a range of tropical diseases. Japanese forces were made up of one tank regiment and six infantry regiments, and were met initially with strong resistance. A counter-attack was launched by units including the 26th Cavalry of the Philippines Scouts, who fought bravely against impossible odds. The fate of Bataan, however, was now sealed and the Filipino-US forces withdrew from one defensive position after another with the Japanese constantly on their tails.

Within a few days the end had come in Bataan and the US command surrendered on 9 April. Following this, 12,000 US and 64,000 Filipino troops were forced to march up to 80 miles to holding camps. During this brutal march 2,300 Americans and 10,000 Filipinos died, often from exhaustion but also by execution when they failed to keep moving. Now the only resistance to the Japanese was from the concrete defences on the island of Corregidor which was garrisoned by 11,000 US-Filipino troops. On Corregidor the defenders suffered heavy bombardments from the air and by the Japanese artillery from 9 April–6 May. In readiness for the assault on the fortress the Japanese commander, General Homma, had ordered all available artillery to be brought up. This included 46 155mm guns, 28 105mm and 32 75mm as well as a few huge 240mm. They took their time sighting the guns with the help of strong intelligence work by the Japanese observers. With no air opposition from the US, a reconnaissance squadron spent hours over the beleaguered fortress. In addition, a balloon company was to be in the air opposite Corregidor to direct artillery fire against it. After weeks of heavy bombardment the Japanese launched an amphibious assault on Corregidor on the night of 5 May. The Japanese assault force suffered horrendous casualties during the landings on the fortress with some units losing 75 per cent of their men. When they managed to bring light tanks ashore the fortress was doomed and it fell just as the Japanese commander was ready to call the attack off. On 6 May General Wainwright, the US commander, surrendered to Homma and his commanders and the Philippines Campaign was over. The conquest of the Philippines had cost the Japanese 12,000 casualties but on paper they had defeated a US-Filipino army of 140,000 men.

On the runway of Del Carmen airfield near Manila a pair of Seversky P-35s lie destroyed after a Japanese air raid. This airfield was attacked at the same time as the Japanese were targeting Clark Field, where the US P-40 fighters were based. Most of the P-35s were destroyed in the Japanese raids but two did survive to fight in the defence of Bataan. One was handed over to the Philippines Army Air Corps (PAAC) and was flown by Captain Ramon Zosa. He flew a sortie on 3 May along with a P-40 fighter against the Japanese landings at Macajalar.

A Japanese Imperial Air Force pilot watches his comrades take off in their fighter aircraft from a recently captured US airfield in northern Luzon. The Imperial Air Force soon established air superiority over the USA destroying most of their P-40 and P-35 fighters on 8 December. P-40 fighters at Clark Field tried to take off but only four got off the ground and were outnumbered by the Japanese Zeros. A whole squadron of P-35 fighters at El Carmen airfield got into the air but these outdated planes were all shot down by the dreaded Japanese fighter.

Japanese troops hunker down in their landing boat as it heads towards the beach at Aparri on the coast of northern Luzon. The 2,000-strong Aparri invasion force, the 'Tanaka Detachment', named after its commander Colonel Tanaka, had sailed from Formosa on 7 December. The troops came ashore on 10 December and faced little opposition from the Philippines troops of the 11th Division in the area. At the same time another 2,000-strong force, the 'Kanno Detachment', was landing at Vigan in northern Luzon in heavy seas.

US soldiers survey the damage done by Japanese Imperial Air Force bombers to the town of Paranique, close to Manila, on 13 December 1941. Once the Japanese had gained air superiority in the skies above the Philippines there was little that the US and Philippines armies could do to counter these raids. At this time the US and Filipino forces were trying to hold back the Japanese before the decision was made to withdraw to the Bataan peninsula.

Japanese troops wade ashore from their landing boat carrying much of the arms and equipment on their backs. On 22 December the main landing of Japanese troops took place in the Lingayen Gulf on the west coast of Luzon. It was covered by the two detachments that had landed further north at Aparri and Vigan on 10 December. Made up of three detachments and two tank units of the 48th Imperial Division, this was to be the main invasion force. The only Filipino units defending the long coast of the gulf were the 11th and 21st Divisions with only one having any artillery.

The shortage of heavy and medium anti-aircraft guns on Luzon meant that lighter weapons like this .50 water cooled machine gun had to be employed. Although this gun was more than capable of shooting down low-flying aircraft, it did not have the range for high-flying bombers. Its four-man Filipino crew may not have received the amount of training necessary to use this gun to its full capability. Training in the Philippines army was inconsistent and some troops were sent to fight after only the most basic of crash courses. Another issue for the troops was the lack of steel helmets as the 120,000 ordered by MacArthur had not arrived in time.

Japanese naval landing force troops cautiously approach a US-held position on Jolo Island, off the coast of Mindanao Island, on 24 December 1941. The Japanese plan was to capture Jolo Island on the western side of Mindanao and Davao Island on the eastern side as a first step in the conquest of the Philippines. Once these two strategic islands were under the control of the Imperial Navy Japanese ships could restrict supplies reaching the largest Philippines island, Luzon. Davao was taken on the 20th and when Jolo fell four days later this first move by the Japanese had been completed. They then concentrated their efforts on attacking Luzon with the conquest of Mindanao left to later in the campaign.

A Type 89 medium tank tries to cross a wooden bridge during the Imperial Army's advance towards Manila. This tank had been the backbone of the Japanese armoured division since the late 1930s but was slow with a top speed of only 25mph. At the start of the campaign there were a total of thirty-four Type 89s serving with the 7th Tank Regiment. During the Philippines Campaign Japanese tanks were to face a number of US M3 Stuart tanks which operated in pairs and were successful in destroying several of the enemy.

The commander of a platoon of Japanese light tanks looks for any signs of enemy movement in the suburbs of Manila. Although the city was declared an 'open city' by the US authorities on 27 December, it was still bombed by the Japanese who had not acknowledged its neutral status. This cynical decision was to make sure that there would be no resistance when their troops entered the city on 31 December.

American troops take cover around a camouflaged machine-gun position which forms part of the northern Bataan defence lines. General MacArthur withdrew his headquarters into the Bataan peninsula on 23 December 1941. A week later on 1 January 1942 all remaining US and Filipino units on Luzon tried to move into Bataan. They set up a first line of defence in the north around Mount Natib but when this line was breached they retreated southwards. In their panic some units even abandoned their rifles as they tried to escape the advancing Japanese. The second defence line was to the north of Mount Marivales and this held until 25 January.

A Japanese Type 97 medium tank moves forward through the jungle of Bataan as the Imperial Army advance continues. This tank was the best available in 1942 and was armed with a 47mm main gun in its turret. During the Philippines Campaign there were only two of the Type 97 available in the 7th Tank Regiment, and these fought alongside larger numbers of the Type 89. The jungles of Bataan were not the best terrain for tanks, although several tank-to-tank encounters took place in this area during the fighting.

Two Type 95 light tanks move past the sharpened bamboo barricade erected by the US and Filipino defenders of the Bataan peninsula. This tank was not particularly well armoured and only had a 37mm main armament but served the Imperial Army until 1945. In total the Japanese had 52 of the Type 95 during the Philippines Campaign, 38 in the 4th Tank Regiment and 14 in the 7th.

Japanese soldiers lie dead in the jungle after a skirmish with US-Filipino forces in the fighting in the Bataan peninsula. The Imperial Army was not always victorious and its soldiers were not all battle-hardened veterans. One Japanese unit, the 65th Brigade, formed in 1941, was made up of second-grade soldiers intended to act as garrison troops. It had to be pushed into action on Bataan with minimal training and without its full complement of machine guns and other weapons. Surprisingly, the 65th was to perform well during the campaign even though its commander had considered it 'unfit for combat'.

US troops and a couple of war correspondents hitch a ride on a White half-track armoured personnel carrier during the fighting on Bataan. These armoured vehicles were deployed with the two tank units in the Philippines, the 192nd and 194th Tank Battalions. The soldier sat on the front of the half-track is armed with a Thompson sub-machine gun with the old-style drum magazine.

Filipino troops prepare to blow a wooden bridge on the Bataan peninsula with sticks of dynamite. The actions of units of dynamiters like these succeeded in slowing the Japanese advance through the peninsula. Although the US and Filipino troops, such as these, were still fighting, their morale was suffering as well as their health. Early in the campaign the defenders were consuming 2,000 calories per day with no fresh fruit or meat. Although water buffalo were hunted by the troops and the 26th Cavalry shot their horses for meat, the ration had been reduced to 1,000 calories by the end of the fighting on Bataan. This level of food rationing was, as the army doctors said, 'barely sufficient to maintain life'.

Troopers of the 26th Cavalry of the Philippines Scouts move along a river during the build up to the war against Japan. The 26th was the last remaining cavalry unit in the US army and was to fight the Philippines Campaign on horseback. In late November 1941 the 26th Cavalry had a strength of 787 Filipinos and 55 US officers. By late December there were only 450 troopers still fighting and these were to launch a number of charges during the fighting. One of these involved a troop of the 26th attacking two Japanese tanks before escaping into the jungle. The last cavalry charge was made by the men of Lieutenant Edwin Ramsey's unit on 16 January at Monong in Bataan. It was a brave but suicidal attack which cost the lives of all the cavalrymen who took part in it.

General MacArthur left the Philippines in March to take up command of the South-West Pacific theatre in Australia. His 'I shall return' defiant speech made him a popular hero in the USA but did not go down as well with his own troops back in the Philippines. Many felt abandoned by their commander and had more affection for his successor, General Wainwright, who shared their captivity until 1945. MacArthur was a complicated character who had many strengths and weaknesses. He also made a few strategic mistakes during the Philippines Campaign and rarely took advice. As one commentator said, 'everything about Douglas MacArthur is on a grand scale; his virtues and triumphs and shortcomings'.

US and Filipino troops share a quick meal in their bivouac during a break from fighting for the Bataan peninsula. The defenders of Bataan were pushed back on several fronts during late March and early April. When the eastern sector of the front held by US-Filipino forces collapsed on 8 April the end was in sight. Their commander, General King, ordered the destruction of all their equipment during the night. Of the 78,000 troops, only 2,000 were successfully evacuated to the fortress of Corregidor on the 9th.

Three of the medical staff in Hospital No. 2 on Bataan, from left to right, Nurse Lieutenant Josephine Nesbitt, Doctor M.C. Davison and Nurse Lieutenant Helen Hennessey. The nurses were known affectionately as the 'Angels of Bataan' or 'Battling Belles of Bataan'. In total there were 11 navy nurses, 66 army nurses and 1 nurse anaesthetist in the military hospitals. Medical staff had to cope with a horrendous list of illnesses as well as the battle injuries of the troops. Malaria, beri beri, dysentery and scurvy were rife as well as other lesser known tropical deceases. By March 500 men per day were being admitted to hospitals for malaria alone and a month later 80 per cent of the defenders had the disease. As many as 75 per cent of the troops had debilitating dysentery symptoms, whilst 35 per cent were suffering from beri beri, and most troops had at least one disease.

This press photograph shows two of the heroes of Bataan, Captain Arthur. W. Wermuth of the US army and his Filipino aide. The original caption for the press photograph says that between them they accounted for 100 dead Japanese during the campaign. In the battle for Bataan the US and Filipino troops, especially those from the Philippines Scouts, fought well together. Captain Wermuth is armed with the ubiquitous Thompson sub-machine whilst his aide has a Smith & Wesson revolver.

COME, FRIENDS!

our life is too precious to loose in
e meaningless war. Quit fighting
ad come like in this picture.
e'll treat you
ood and right.

This Japanese propaganda leaflet dropped over Filipino lines during the campaign is straightforward in its message to troops of the Philippines army. It states why fight in a 'meaningless war' on behalf of the USA when we will treat anyone who comes over to us well. The Japanese saw themselves as the leaders of all Asian peoples but in most cases they simply replaced European colonial power with their often harsher version.

Bicycles were used in large numbers by the Japanese in Malaya, the Netherlands East Indies and also in the Philippines. Here a bicycle unit moves through the jungle across hastily constructed walkways during the advance on Manila. During the Philippines Campaign one bicycle unit was decimated due to its soldiers' obsession with protecting their precious cycles. In late December 1941 a 300-strong unit of cyclists was trapped on a road on Luzon by a well-organized US and Filipino ambush. Rather than abandon their bicycles and head for cover, they rode them through heavy fire and turned around to ride out of the ambush. This foolish act resulted in the deaths of 250 of the men in the unit who died trying to protect their bicycles. A similar incident had happened during the Malayan Campaign when 150 soldiers were killed riding their bicycles through heavy fire rather than leaving them behind.

Japanese soldiers rush from behind the cover of a wrecked tank across open ground towards US trenches on the Bataan peninsula. Even during their victorious advance through South-East Asia and the Pacific, the Imperial Army sometimes employed suicidal banzai attacks. On Bataan at midnight of 10 January repeated attempts were made to breach Filipino defensive positions. This involved Imperial Army soldiers throwing themselves at barbed wire so that their comrades could climb over their dead bodies. The desperation of the attack was a sign of tactics to be used more and more frequently from 1943–5 as the war turned against Japan.

A US marine master sergeant explains the finer points of a Lewis machine-gun magazine to a group of Filipino troops on Corregidor Island in early May 1942. When the fighting began there was a shortage of light machine guns in the Philippines army. There was only one Browning heavy automatic rifle per Filipino company whilst US companies had eight. These men look intently at the NCO whilst his comrade checks his steel helmet for any damage. Headgear and uniforms amongst the Filipinos varies with a mix of steel helmets and garrison caps worn with various shades of khaki.

The US crew of an anti-aircraft gun of the 200th Coastal Artillery of the New Mexico National Guard man their gun on Bataan. This unit was effectively part of the second-line territorial force of the USA but specialist crews like this were desperately needed in time of war and were now expected to put their training back in the USA into effect. When they arrived in the Philippines the 200th Coastal had twenty-four 37mm anti-aircraft guns and then received further guns. However, by the time the fighting began seven of their anti-aircraft guns had been sent to Manila for repairs.

As the original caption to this press photograph says, 'the Japanese did not have all their own way'. A US soldier and his Filipino comrades bring into their lines a sorry looking group of Japanese troops after a skirmish on Bataan. It was very unusual for Imperial Army troops to surrender at any time during the war and these men may belong to a labour unit. During the war in Nomonhan against the Soviet Union in 1939 any prisoners who returned to Japan were shunned by their family and friends and many were pressured into committing suicide.

Confident Philippines Scouts celebrate a local victory against Japanese troops who had landed on the western coast of the Bataan peninsula. The photograph says that it was taken on 10 April but it was probably taken a few days before. One of the Scouts is showing off his war booty Samurai taken from the body of a dead Imperial Army officer during the fighting. Another of his comrades holds a Model 32 Japanese steel helmet with camouflage netting.

Defeated US and Filipino troops are lined up ready for their 'death march' from Bataan to Cabanoatuan, 75 miles away. What happened during the march was a mixture of lack of preparation and incompetence by the Japanese and sheer brutality as thousands died from exhaustion, hunger or by execution. The Japanese had only expected to take 40,000 prisoners of war and had insufficient food or water for them. As the prisoners struggled forward any stragglers, wounded or anyone who accepted food or water from the local population was killed out of hand. Estimates of the numbers who died during the march vary greatly largely due to the confusion at the time but at least 5,650 but probably nearer to the higher estimate of 18,000 died.

US army officers and men look on with terror at the unseen Japanese soldiers looming over them during the death march. As these and other Allied prisoners were to find out during their 1942–5 captivity, their lives depended on the whim of their captors. During the march many were bayoneted or killed with Samurai swords for the slightest indiscretion. As so many of the prisoners were ill with various tropical diseases, many of them simply couldn't keep up with the column and were killed by their guards.

A Japanese artillery piece fires towards Corregidor Island from the southern coast of the Bataan peninsula. From 9 April until the beginning of May the Japanese guns relentlessly bombarded the isolated fortress in Manila Bay. Inside the well-protected concrete bunkers of the fortress the morale of the defenders remained high even though any thoughts of relief had ended. The US and Filipino garrisons were now determined to resist for as long as possible even if only to delay the final Japanese victory.

This photograph shows a Japanese 70mm howitzer firing from close range at the defences of Corriegidor. Once the Japanese had landed troops on the island it was only a matter of time before the end came. The first landing by Japanese troops on the island on 5 May was costly for the attackers and 800 of the 2,000-strong force were killed. The surviving Japanese, with the support of a few artillery pieces and three tanks, wore down the defenders' resistance. With no anti-tank guns in the defenders' armoury, the Japanese tanks were to be decisive in the fall of Corriegidor.

The soldiers who won the battle for the US fortress of Corriegidor perform a banzai in celebration of their hard-won victory. Behind them is one of the large guns that had protected the island from attack in what proved to be a futile if gallant effort. Japanese casualties in the taking of Corriegidor were heavy and at times it looked like the assault force was going to be overwhelmed by the defenders. When the fortress fell on 7 May 11,000 exhausted US and 4,000 Filipino troops were taken prisoner.

A flag bearer of the Japanese naval landing forces poses on a hillside on the Philippines island of Mindanao in May 1942. Whilst the battle for the Bataan peninsula continued and then Corregidor Island, Filipino forces carried on fighting on Mindanao. They were still fighting in parts of the large island when General Wainwright announced the surrender of all US and Filipino forces on 7 May. This announcement, broadcast from Manila, included all the forces who were continuing to fight on Mindanao and other Philippines islands.

General Yamashita, the conqueror of Malaya, wearing the cork sun helmet welcomes his counterpart, General Sugiyama, to the Philippines in the rain. Yamashita was one of the most intelligent of Japan's generals and was part of the detailed planning team for the 'Strike South' group on the island of Formosa from 1940. This group put some Japanese troops through jungle training in the jungles of the island in preparation for the attack on Malaya. Sugiyama had also been one of the main advocates of the 'Strike South' policy and was against an attack on the Soviet Union. He had told Emperor Hirohito that Japan could 'probably' win a war against Britain, the USA and the Netherlands in five months.

Chapter Ten

The Burma Campaign, December 1941– February 1942

At the start of the war in South-East Asia the British possession of Burma was not involved for a month apart from several large-scale air raids on Rangoon, the capital. Burma had been a British possession since 1885 when it was annexed after hard fighting against the Burmese population. Most Burmese never really accepted British rule and the majority Burmese population was not trusted to serve in the military. Most of the work in Burma was also done by 1 million southern Indians who worked in the factories and docks. The Burmese population more or less got on with their lives ignoring when possible the fact that they were under British rule. Burma had been governed as a province of India until 1937 and the Indian army had responsibility for its defence.

In 1940 the garrison in Burma was intended for internal security only with six infantry battalions available. Two of these were British and the other four made up of the Burma Rifles were recruited from ethnic minorities like the Kachin, China and Karen tribes. In May 1941 the Burmese population had finally been given permission to join the British Indian Army but few volunteered. Generally morale was low in the Burmese units and service in them was unpopular with the British officers seconded to them. In most cases officers constantly applied to be transferred back to their British or Indian army unit. In an effort to beef up the Burmese defence forces the four original battalions of Burma Rifles were doubled in 1940 to eight, but this move only reduced their standard. In preparation for any Japanese attack a 1st Burma Division was formed from two brigades of Burma Rifles and the 14th Indian Brigade to try and improve performance. On 12 December the Burmese defence was reinforced by the arrival of the 16,000-strong 17th 'Black Cat' Indian Division from Iraq. This division was to be almost solely responsible for the defence of Burma during the first months of the campaign. It arrived from Iraq trained for desert warfare and totally untrained for the jungle warfare that it was about to face.

The first clash between the Japanese and Indian forces took place in the far south of Burma in mid-December. Victoria Point on the Burmese-Thai border and its airfield was seized by the Japanese on 15 December 1941. Burma did not really interest the Japanese war planners and the only reason they might want to conquer it was to protect the north-west flank of their projected 'Greater East Asian Co-Prosperity Sphere'. From the British point of view their main reason for defending Burma was in order to keep Nationalist China in the war against Japan. Winston Churchill was also determined that Burma should be defended so that the important Indian north-eastern cities like Calcutta could be protected from Japanese air attack. Burma's defence had been the responsibility of India before 1937 but from then until the outbreak of the Second World war they were responsible for their own defence. From 1939 until November 1940 Burma was put under the control of the authorities in London before being incorporated into the Far Eastern Command. The local military commanders called for Burma to be returned to Indian authority and this happened on 12 December 1941, but only lasted a few weeks. On 30 December Burma was put under ABDA command and then when the Netherlands East Indies fell it was returned to Indian protection.

The Japanese force given the task of conquering Burma was the 15th Army which had been responsible for protecting the flank of the 25th Army during its advance into Malaya. Now that the campaign in Malaya was progressing nicely the 15th, whose 35,440 troops were veterans from China, was released to begin its own offensive into south-eastern Burma. On 12 January 1942 the 15th Army struck unexpectedly from south-western Thailand into southern Burma. The invasion force was made up initially of two infantry divisions under the command of General Shojiro Iido.

British troops in Burma were under the command of General Thomas Hutton and comprised a diverse force of about one-and-a-half divisions. These British, Indian and Burmese troops were poorly trained and were not really prepared to fight a battle-hardened army. The first major battle took place at Moulmein in southern Burma and lasted for two days from 29–31 January. British forces withdrawing from their defeat at Moulmein had to face crossing the wide Salween River in the hope of preparing defences on the other side. However, the Japanese had advanced quickly and outflanked the defences and crossed the river further north and now threatened to encircle the British. The defeated British forces then began another withdrawal to the Sittang River but were caught by the rapidly advancing Japanese at Bilin on 18 February, and a five-day battle ensued. Disaster now struck for the British as the only bridge across the Sittang was threatened by the Japanese on the 23rd in yet another flanking move. In desperation the British blew the bridge trapping thousands of their troops on the other side. Although some soldiers did manage to swim over the river to safety, many more fell into Japanese hands and all of their heavy equipment was lost. The defeat at Sittang cost the British 5,000 men and 6,000 weapons with just 3,484 troops managing to get across the river to temporary safety. The sacrifice of the British troops and equipment was justified at the time by the fact that if the bridge remained intact it would have allowed the Japanese to destroy most of the British forces in central Burma.

A ground crew at a Imperial Navy Air Force base prepares to load bombs on to their Mitsubishi G4M medium bomber. This was one of the main medium bombers in service with the Japanese along with the G3M and the KI-21 and served from 1941 until the end of the war. At the time of Pearl Harbor there were 200 of the G4M in service and it was scheduled to replace the G3M. The crew are chalking suitably patriotic messages on the bombs before loading them into the bomb bay. KI-21s could carry up to 2,200lb of bombs

Japanese Mitsubishi G3M2 attack bombers fly over Rangoon during one of their devastating raids on the city and its port facilities. Heavy bombing on 23 and 25 December 1941 resulted in the deaths of 2,500 people with a similar number injured. It was reported that many Burmese and Indians came out to watch the first air raid before the reality of what was happening dawned on them. The Japanese had filled some bombs with shrapnel to increase the number of civilian casualties and cause maximum panic. About 100,000 Indian port workers fled the city to the safety of the countryside virtually shutting down Rangoon port until they returned. When the raids subsided the port went back to normal operations and continued until the city fell in March 1942.

Although this photograph shows a platoon of Japanese troops charging up a hill in Burma in early 1942, it could be anywhere in South-East Asia in 1941–2. On 16 January 1942 the Japanese 16th Battalion crossed the border from northern Thailand and captured the strategic Victoria Point in south-eastern Burma. They faced no opposition as the British garrison had already been withdrawn to new positions to the north-west.

Japanese troops of the 15th Army cross the border between Thailand and Burma at the start of their offensive towards the Burmese capital Rangoon. The plan had been for the 15th Army to guard the flank of the 25th Army as it invaded Malaya. Once the fighting in Malaya reached a favourable point it was to be released to begin its own campaign to conquer Burma. Its objective was to capture southern Burma along the Rahong–Moulmein route eventually reaching Rangoon. To help in this campaign the 15th was now reinforced with the Imperial Army's Guard Division.

Japanese troops move forward during their advance through southern Burma in early 1942. They progressed using any available cover, as they had been trained to do in the months leading up to the outbreak of war. Some Japanese troops had been given specialist training in jungle and night fighting in Formosa. Their night-fighting training involved being able to recognize the sounds of the jungle and distinguish between them and sounds of enemy troops. They were also trained to wrap their bayonet and other kit in cloth to avoid any clattering or flashing metal as they moved forward. Troops also wrapped their hobnail boots in cloth so that the nails did not catch any light.

British soldiers of the 2nd Battalion King's Own Yorkshire Regiment move through jungle just before the Japanese invasion. The 2nd Battalion had been in Burma since 1936 and had been at the back of the queue when it came to new weapons, equipment and uniform. During the Burma Campaign only eighty of the battalion were ready for service and these had lost their heavy machine guns, which had been taken for airfield defence. With no steel helmets, they were issued with India pattern cork solar topees which were only seen in service in Burma in 1941–2.

A lone Burmese sentry stands guard over a field of punji sticks made from sharpened bamboo which were intended to repel Japanese paratroopers. He is guarding the perimeter of one of the airfields built by the British in southern Burma which acted as a transit stop for aircraft flying between India and Malaya. Four of these strategic airfields were in Tenasserim province which was dangerously close to the border with Thailand, only 60 miles away.

Soldiers of the Burma Rifles are using a Vickers M1912 heavy machine gun in the anti-aircraft role during jungle training. They wear the distinctive bush hat with the left brim pinned up with the badge of their regiment on it. The Burma Rifles were the best trained of the Burmese troops fighting in 1941–2 and were recruited from the ethnic minorities of the country. During the Burma Campaign they were at a distinct disadvantage as orders were usually issued to them by their Indian officers in Hindustani.

Some Japanese troops advanced northwards from Martaban in late February 1942 using elephants to transport themselves and their equipment. The Japanese Imperial Army had always shown its resourcefulness in using whatever form of transport was available. Because of the shortage of elephants only a limited number of troops could travel in this way. These soldiers are having to rely on the elephants' howdahs to control them so only one or two soldiers could be carried.

Burmese Frontier Force cavalry move up to the front during fighting with the Japanese in early 1942. These Indian troopers of the BFF appear to be Sikhs who had been seconded from some of the many horse regiments of the Indian army. Although these men appear to have reasonable horses, a shortage of good mounts meant that some BFF troopers had to go into action riding small but hardy Burmese ponies. An eyewitness said that the tall Indian troopers feet almost trailed on the ground as they rode through his village.

A pair of US-built Brewster F2A-3 Buffalo fighters of the RAF take off from a Burmese airfield to bravely try and counter the superior Japanese fighters such as the KI-43. The delay by the US authorities in getting the Brewster into front-line service meant that it was virtually obsolescent by 1941. Perhaps the British dependence on the Buffalo sums up the situation faced by their military forces in the Far East. They were often given the equipment that was deemed to be too old or worn for other theatres of war. After all, they were only fighting the Japanese whose planes were regarded by some as second-class 'copies' of other nations' aircraft. As one senior RAF officer had said before the fighting in Malaya, 'We can get on with the Buffaloes out here'. He said that England needed the Spitfires and that 'Buffaloes are quite good enough for Malaya'.

Indian 3in mortar crewmen of the 17th Division in pre-war training for the coming campaign when their unit was to be the backbone of the British army in Burma. By February 1942 the 17th had been pushed back from its defensive lines on the Salween River in southern Burma. When the three brigades withdrew again to the Sittang River they were faced with disaster as the only bridge over the river had been blown up. This terrible decision had been taken in the confusion of the fighting and meant that the 17th was trapped. With the advancing Japanese behind them, 3,300 Indian troops tried to cross the fast-flowing river. Although the survivors of the crossing were able to join up with other units at Pegu, the disaster at the Sittang Bridge broke their fighting spirit.

A Japanese unit advances through a Burmese village in February 1942. The inhabitants have been moved out of their homes whilst the troops passed through. The Burmese population was largely indifferent to who ruled them as one colonial power was much the same as another. Some joined the Japanese army as auxiliaries but most just wanted to be left alone by the combatants. The majority of Burmese people had little loyalty to the British Empire but had little hope of a better life under the Japanese Empire.

The Japanese machine-gun crew of a 7.7mm Type 92 fires from cover towards British lines during the Burma Campaign. Japanese troops nearly always camouflaged themselves and their weapons during combat and many were masters of concealment. Their Allied foes were slow to learn this lesson during their chaotic defence of Burma in 1941–2. When both sides fought again in Burma from 1943 until 1945 most of the advantages that the Japanese had had in the previous campaign had disappeared.

Chapter Eleven

The Burma Campaign,
March–May 1942

In early March Major General William Slim was sent from Iraq to try and create a new military force which might be able to counter the Japanese. He combined the remaining units of the 17th Indian Division and the poorly equipped 1st Burma Division to create the 1st Burma Corps, or Burcorps. This new formation was bolstered by the arrival of the 7th Armoured Brigade made up of the 7th Hussars and 2nd Royal Tank Regiment, which were veterans of the North African Campaign. The arrival of the 7th Brigade brought the British forces up to a strength of two ad-hoc divisions. Other reinforcements for the British army in Burma came from the East when Chinese Nationalist armies crossed the border from China during February and March. The initial Chinese Nationalist offer of troops to fight in Burma was politely turned down by General Wavell. Chiang Kai-shek had offered the Nationalist 5th and 6th Armies but Wavell was worried that the Nationalist Army's lack of a supply system would mean that the Chinese troops would have to 'live off the land'. He did accept the 93rd Division of the 6th Army but as a Nationalist division was only the size of a British regiment this was only a token force but the number of Chinese troops rose to 30,000 men. The Chinese took up their positions around the city of Toungoo on 19 March to protect the Burma Road.

Meanwhile, the Japanese had crossed the Sittang River and were advancing rapidly towards the two major cities of Pegu and Rangoon. Rangoon was abandoned by the British on 7 March and Pegu fell on the 5th followed by Rangoon on the 8th. General Alexander, of North African Campaign fame, was now brought in to relieve General Hutton of his thankless task. After a lull in the fighting the Japanese struck at the Chinese forces at Toungoo on the 21st forcing them to withdraw before they were totally surrounded. British forces now retreated north of the city of Prome to protect the oilfields at Yenangyuang.

In late March Japanese reinforcements arrived by sea at newly captured Rangoon and these were made up of two divisions fresh from victory in Malaya. In addition, they received 200 aircraft released from successful campaigns elsewhere bringing the total available up to 600. With these new troops and planes General Iida could now advance into central Burma and try and end the fighting before the demoralized British could regroup.

The British forces in Burma were on the verge of capitulation by April 1942 having faced a series of defeats at the hands of the Japanese 15th Army since early January. On 11 April the Japanese sent a reinforced division against the British defending the oilfields at Yenangyuang. The oilfields were away from the paddy fields and jungle of southern Burma in what was called the 'dry zone' of Burma. Japanese units broke through the 1st Burma Division's defences on the 13th and pushed them back into their inner defences. Not for the first time the British forces had been outflanked and virtually encircled by the advancing Japanese. General Stilwell then ordered his 38th Chinese Division to march southwards to relieve the besieged forces at Yenangyuang. The fighting around Yenangyuang was some of the most bitter of the campaign especially as it was fought in 114 degrees of heat. Soldiers ran out of water and some resorted to drinking from the radiators of their trucks in desperation. British engineers, meanwhile, destroyed any useful equipment at the oilfields which the Japanese had hoped to capture intact. The British forces managed to escape from Yenangyuang largely due to the casualties suffered by the Japanese fighting against the 'elite' 38th Division.

The Japanese then sent the 56th Division with a regiment of tanks against the Chinese 6th Army near Taunggyi. This destroyed one Chinese division and forced the 6th Army to retire to the north before crossing back into Yunnan province. Lashio, the terminus of the Burma Road to China, fell to the Japanese on 29 April and the British withdrew to a new defensive line further north. By late April the whole of central Burma was in Japanese hands and the campaign now became a fighting retreat by the British. Mandalay, which was defended by 60,000 British and Indian troops and the Chinese 22nd Division, fell on 1 May. Forces escaping from Mandalay retreated towards Myitkyina in northern Burma. A British three-brigade counter-attack against the recently captured town of Mongya failed and caused a further withdrawal westwards to Shywegyin, close to the Indian border. The defeat of the British at Shywegyin on 3 May saw the withdrawal of 20,000 British troops, 74 guns and thousands of civilians. Whilst they tried to escape by river steamer, the Japanese air force strafed the helpless civilians causing further chaos. Over the next few days the Japanese took Bhamo on the 4th and on the 6th forced the withdrawal of the Chinese 200th Division and part of the 55th Division from their positions at Taunggyi. On 8 May the northern town of Myitkyina was captured by the Japanese who then continued their advance towards the Indian border. Two days later they captured Kalewa in the west of Burma and again progressed to the Indian border.

By mid-May the end was in sight for the British army in Burma and the first of their retreating units reached Assam province across the Indian border on the 14th. On 12 May the Japanese had crossed the Salween River in the east of Burma and advanced on the Chinese-Burma border town of Kengtung, which they took on the 28th. By 20 May the Japanese were in full control of the vast majority of Burma and only had to mop up any continuing resistance. The British, Indian and Chinese units had been making for the safety of the Chinese border in the east and Indian border in the north-west since mid-May. General Stilwell and some of his Chinese troops could not get to China and had to walk all the way to India instead. The British 1,250-mile retreat through central and northern Burma was the longest in their military history. Although Burma had been lost temporarily, a total of 12,000 men had got out hopefully to fight another day. They had, however, left all their heavy equipment behind and arrived in India riddled with lice and suffering with typhus with most also having contracted malaria. The majority would not be fit to return to the conflict until they had had a long recuperation and many would never be fit enough to fight in the front line. Japanese losses in the conquest of Burma were 4,597 whilst the defeated British, Indian and Burmese troops lost 13,463 troops in the fighting.

Imperial Army troops trudge wearily into the centre of Rangoon which fell to them on 8 March. The city had been evacuated the day before with the withdrawing British forces moving northwards having to depend on air supply. As the Japanese advanced into the Burmese capital some of their units were positioned to stop the evacuation. An Indian infantry force with tanks and artillery support broke through the encirclement allowing the evacuation to continue.

Indian cavalry of the BFF patrol the rugged border between Burma and Thailand. The mounted branch of the BFF was organized into a reconnaissance force which was divided into independent columns of about 60–100 sabres each. These columns were headed by young, less well-off Indian army officers such as Captain A.G. Sandeman, 'Sandy', of the Central India Horse. These officers had often joined the BFF because of the higher rates of pay they received than in their old regiments.

Sandeman commanded his column during the fighting around Toungoo in March 1942 and on the 21st he led his men into their last action. In the confused situation around Toungoo he mistook a Japanese unit for Chinese Nationalist troops. When he realized his mistake some of his men went to inform a nearby mountain gun battery of the enemy position. About half of his mixed Sikh and Punjabi column then charged the well dug-in Japanese troops. In what is regarded as the last cavalry charge in history, his troopers, shouting the Sikh battle cry 'Sat Sri Akal', followed Sandeman to their deaths. Their courageous but suicidal charge ended with the deaths of all of the troopers involved.

Indian gunners are seen manning their Bofors 40mm anti-aircraft gun at the town of Tailingdwingyi. According to the original caption, these same gunners shot down a Japanese medium bomber shortly after the photograph was taken. The gun is kept well camouflaged with jungle foliage until needed by the crew wearing a mixture of turbans and steel helmets. This suggests that the men are a mixture of Hindus and Sikhs serving in the same gun crew.

A Chinese Nationalist soldier rushes through the Burmese bush during an attack against the Japanese in central Burma at Pyu to the south of Toungoo in March 1942. He is cradling his Mauser rifle with bayonet fixed under his arm trying to avoid snagging it on the undergrowth. The Chinese forces in Burma had come under the command of Major General Joseph W. Stilwell, who arrived at the front on 14 March. Stilwell had been acting as military advisor to the Chinese leader Chiang Kai-shek and was known as 'Vinegar Joe' because of his forthright attitude which did not endear him to many Chinese officers.

A patrol of Chinese Nationalist soldiers moves into the jungle around the city of Toungoo which their 5th and 6th Armies had been ordered to defend. Despite the reluctance by the British to accept help from the Chinese some units of the Nationalist Army often put up a good fight, especially in defence. However, the attitude of some Nationalist officers greatly frustrated their Allies in 1942. They had been trained to avoid losing precious weaponry and equipment in battle and this led to them avoiding combat at times. This was not because they were cowards but because in their experience in fighting from 1937–42, once weapons were lost they were never replaced.

Two Chinese Nationalist soldiers of the Expeditionary Army sent by Chiang Kai-shek to Burma stand guard over a suspected Burmese agitator. He had been accused of helping the invading Japanese and may have faced swift justice from his Chinese captors. The average Burmese was at best indifferent to the fate of the Allies in 1942 and many supported the Japanese. Most had no real loyalty to the British Empire and there had been several rebellions against British rule in the 1930s. The fear of the British and Dutch authorities of attacks by revolutionary elements amongst the populations of their colonies was another hindrance to their defence.

Russian supplied T-26B light tanks of the 200th Mechanized Division of the Chinese Nationalist Army are seen on the Burmese–Chinese border. When the 'elite' 200th Division went into Burma to support the British it is not known how many of their eighty T-26s went with them. Photographs indicate, however, that a number of French AMR Renault light tanks did serve with the 200th Division in Burma in 1942. They, like any T-26s, would have probably been lost during their retreat back into China at the end of the campaign.

The pilots of Curtiss P-40 Tomahawks of the American Volunteer Group of the Chinese Nationalist Air Force leave their planes after a sortie. A squadron of these planes was loaned to the British in Burma during the 1942 fighting by Chiang Kai-shek. This type of plane had been flown for several months by the American Volunteer Group over western China before they were moved to Burma. During this period the already experienced US pilots learnt tactics to deal with the various fighters in service with the Japanese. On 21 March 1942 the American Volunteer Group's main base at Magwe was destroyed by Japanese bombers. This meant that the Americans were forced to move back into China and continue their fight from there.

Air Vice Marshal D.F. Stevenson, CBE, DSO, MC, the man in charge of the RAF in Burma, at his Burmese HQ in April. By this stage in the campaign he had few aircraft to command having had at the start of the campaign fory-six Hawker Hurricanes and Brewster Buffaloes. He also had the support of twenty-one P-40s of the American Volunteer Group to support his force. They faced three air regiments of the Japanese 10th Air Brigade with KI-27 fighters, KI-30 attack bombers and KI-21 medium bombers.

Happy and confident Japanese Imperial Army fighter pilots relax between missions during the fighting in Burma in front of a Nakajima KI-43 'Hayabusa' fighter. The Japanese faced little opposition from the RAF in Burma, which only had 50 aged fighters compared with their 150 aircraft at the start of the campaign. The Japanese 5th Air Division was reinforced during the campaign and by the end of the fighting had a total of 400 planes. Originally destined for Singapore, thirty Hurricane fighters were used to bolster the RAF in Burma but these were not enough to tip the balance.

Lieutenant General T.J. Hutton, the British officer in charge of the Burma Command, is seen in conference with his Chinese allies on 15 April 1942. He is talking to Nationalist Chinese General Sun Li-jen, the commander of the 38th Division. Sun was one of the best and brightest commanders in the Nationalist Army and his division reflected that. He proved that the Chinese soldier, if well led, well treated and well armed, could be a match for any other. Unfortunately, competent commanders such as Sun were the exception not the rule in the Chinese Nationalist Army in 1942.

Two Gurhkas manhandle Burmese civilians who have been behaving suspiciously in the eyes of their captors close to the oilfields of Yenangyuang in April 1942. As any Burmese adult male was treated with suspicion, the two men have been blindfolded by their captors. The demoralized British and Indian troops would often act in a heavy handed way with the local population. Fifth columnists were seen everywhere by the jittery Allied soldiers and they acted accordingly. This kind of treatment obviously did not endear the British army to the Burmese people and many greeted the advancing Japanese troops as liberators.

In this well-known Japanese propaganda photograph Imperial Army infantry and machine guns of the 33rd Division move cautiously forward past the destroyed oil derricks of Yenangyuang. The order to destroy the oilfield had been given on 15 April by General Slim to his 1st Burma Division. His men then had to defend their position surrounded by burning oil whilst being bombed by Japanese planes from above. Appeals to the nearest Chinese Nationalist division, the 38th, to come to the relief of the beleaguered defenders were ignored, not by the division's commander but by his superior, General Lo Cho-ying, the head of the Nationalist Expeditionary Corps. When he received the instruction not to assist the British, the 38th Division commander, General Su Li-jen, ignored it and sent his 113th Regiment to help. Su Li-jen was one of the most able of the Chinese commanders in 1942 and was to go on to command Nationalist forces in Burma from 1944–5.

Chinese Nationalist troops of the 38th Division clamber over the hull of a Stuart M3 light tank of the 7th Armoured Brigade at Yenangyuang. The experienced British tankers were veterans of the North African desert campaign and were confident in their abilities. They had little respect for their Japanese counterparts even though they had seen service in Malaya. One tank commander of the 7th Hussars commented that Japanese tankers' battle practice was 'abysmal'. He said that, 'They appeared to be lonely and untrained, and obviously did not know what to do, remaining stationary in the middle of an open field. They were knocked out immediately before they knew we were there'.

In another well-known photograph Japanese troops are seen destroying a British M3 Stuart light tank. According to the description of the encounter, a Major Mugita destroyed the tank using a Molotov cocktail. In the background two Japanese soldiers charge up to the tank to throw their homemade bombs at it whilst their comrades watch from the cover of the jungle. The ferocity and often suicidal bravery of the Japanese Imperial Army was shocking to the British soldier. Japanese soldiers would often gladly sacrifice their lives for the emperor if it was deemed necessary to do so.

Indian troops take part in last-minute training in Mandalay where 60,000 Allied troops were concentrated to defend the city. The Indian formations varied greatly in their training and many reinforcement units were of poorer quality than the original ones. When the 16th Indian Brigade arrived in Burma it had already been stripped of its better troops. These had been sent to fight in other theatres such as North Africa which were given a higher priority than the Far East Campaign. The 16th Brigade's ranks had been filled out with new raw recruits only three days before embarkation!

This highly stylized cover of an Italian newspaper of the period describes the achievements of Italy's ally Japan in taking the city of Mandalay on 1 May 1942. The Japanese Imperial Army entered the city after the Chinese 22nd Division withdrew on 30 April having covered the Allied retreat northwards. By this date all of central Burma was in Japanese hands and a new defensive line was being established. In the meantime, a three-brigade strong British counter-attack to try and capture the city of Monywa failed and this led to further retreats.

LA DOMENICA DEL CORRIERE

Le vittorie dei Giapponesi in Birmania. Occupate le città di Lascio e di Mandalay, le truppe nipponiche proseguono nella loro avanzata. L'automobile di un Comando e i soldati, mimetizzati con foglie di palma per rendersi meno visibili all'aviazione nemica, attraversano una località dove ha infuriato la battaglia. *(Disegno di A. Beltrame)*

Japanese troops cross a small river in upper Burma during their pursuit of the retreating Allied armies in mid-1942. The Japanese 56th Division advanced through the Shan States of Burma reaching Myitkyina in the far north on 8 May. Two other divisions, the 18th and the 33rd, advanced through central and western Burma respectively. Troops of the 33rd Division were close to the border with India in early May whilst those of the 18th Division passed through Mandalay on 1 May. Having chased the British and Chinese forces out of Burma the conquest was complete and another great Japanese victory had been achieved.

A battery of Imperial Army 150mm Type 96s fire from their camouflaged positions during the Burma Campaign. The Type 96 was one of the most modern artillery pieces in service with the Japanese in 1941–2. It had been introduced in 1936 to replace the Type 4 of 1915 vintage, which remained in service until 1945. With a range of 11,850m, it was 2,300m longer than the earlier gun largely because its shell was lighter.

An Imperial Army medium artillery piece fires towards British positions during fighting in northern Burma. The gun is a 105mm Type 91 which was modelled on a French Schneider that the Japanese bought in the 1920s. It was popular but was renowned for its crude finish, although this did not stop it from giving good service to the Imperial Army until 1945.

After the defeat in central Burma a new line of defence was established at Shywegin in northern Burma, but there was little confidence in its ability to hold the Japanese. During the battle for Shywegin on 10 May these ethnic Koumaoni soldiers of the Indian army defended their trench against Japanese attack. The Indian forces at Shywegin did, however, manage to delay the Japanese advance long enough for the retreating British to gain ground on the pursuing Imperial Army. The Kuomaoni people from northern India, who made up several units in the Indian army, were closely related to the Gurhkas of Nepal and shared their fighting spirit.

General Stilwell, the US commander of the Chinese Nationalist Army, leads his HQ staff out of Burma into India in May 1942. Having realized that he could be of no further use to the Allies, Stilwell decided on 1 May to withdraw. He and most of his 100 companions travelled the first 250 miles by jeep and truck before continuing on foot for another 150 miles. The second epic leg of the retreat took fourteen days over mountains and through steamy jungle before they finally arrived at the India–Burma border town of Imphal. During the long retreat the defiant Stilwell was quoted as saying, 'We got a hell of a beating. We got run out of Burma and it is humiliating. We ought to find out why it happened, go back and retake it!'

Doctor Seagrave, the missionary doctor who had been attached to Stilwell's command during the fighting in Burma, treats an officer's ulcerated legs during the march into India. Seagrave and nineteen of his Burmese nurses accompanied the retreating British, Indian, Chinese and Burmese military and civilians. When they reached the safety of India they were surprised to receive a cold reception from the British Indian authorities. The British officers who had not served in Burma unjustly believed that their comrades had 'let the side down' during the 1941–2 fighting.

Burmese Independence Army volunteers parade for their Japanese advisors during their advance through Burma in 1942. The Burmese Independence Army was armed with 1,000 captured British Lee–Enfield .303 rifles and 100 pistols and wore a quasi-military uniform including shop-bought solar topees and trilbys. They marched behind green, yellow and red flags bearing the peacock symbol of pre-British-rule Burma. Young Burmese from the majority Burmese population had been excluded almost totally from British military service. When the Japanese offered them the chance to fight they came forward in their thousands revealing their dormant martial spirit.

A Japanese soldier looks down from the hills above the Salween Gorge, which formed the border between Burma and south-western China. When part of the Chinese Nationalist Army's Expeditionary Force retreated back into Yunnan province the Japanese pursued them for a while. In reality, the Japanese Imperial Army had enough troops already committed to the defeat of China. Any divisions in Burma would have to be ready for an eventual British counter-attack, although this looked unlikely in May 1942.

Chapter Twelve

The War at Sea,
December 1941–May 1942

With the US Pacific Fleet largely put out of action after the attack on Pearl Harbor it was now down to the British, Australian, Dutch and a few US navy ships to counter the Japanese navy. The British had neglected their naval forces in the Far East and had concentrated on the Mediterranean theatre in 1941. In an effort to redress the balance in December 1941 the British had despatched two powerful battleships, HMS *Prince of Wales* and HMS *Repulse*. These mighty vessels and their escort destroyers, HMS *Electra*, HMS *Express*, HMS *Vampire* and HMS *Tenedos*, formed 'Z Force'. Z Force arrived in Singapore and on 8 December was ordered to sail up the east coast of Malaya to the north to attack the Japanese forces landing there. Fatally for the two battleships, they had no air cover and were dependent on land-based RAF aircraft stationed in northern Malaya. The intended air cover was to have been supplied originally by the aircraft carrier HMS *Indomitable*, but she was in port in Jamaica having sustained damage earlier in the month. It was then discovered that the RAF aircraft could not provide air cover for HMS *Prince of Wales* and HMS *Repulse* as their airfields had already been overrun by the Japanese advance. Regardless of the facts, the British commander, Admiral Sir Tom Philips, decided to carry on with his mission even though it was now virtually suicidal. The two ships soon came under massive air attacks from Japanese planes flying from their bases in Indo-China. After 2 hours of constant bombardment both ships were sunk with heavy loss of life leaving the British in the Far East temporarily without a viable naval force.

As a result of the loss of Allied surface ships in late 1941 and early 1942 their submarines took on an important role during the fighting. Although the Royal Navy had had fifteen submarines in the Far East in September 1939, these were withdrawn to the Mediterranean before December 1941. This move illustrates the British obsession with the Mediterranean and North Africa during the build up to the Japanese offensive. The Dutch did, however, have fifteen outdated submarines in the Far East and these fought in the defence of Malaya. Their fleet also suffered heavy losses with only two submarines surviving to defend the Netherlands East Indies in 1942. The US navy had fifty-five fleet-

and eighteen medium-sized submarines in the Pacific in December 1941. These took part in a number of missions during 1941–2. Near the end of the campaign two of the Royal Navy submarines were transferred from the Mediterranean and joined in the defence of the Netherlands East Indies.

Whilst the fighting was going so badly for the Allied armies in Malaya, Burma and the Philippines, at sea the situation was no better. By early 1942 the only useful function for the various British, Dutch, Australian and US ships in the Far East was to try and halt the Japanese invasion of the Netherlands East Indies. One of the few successes for the Allies during this period was the attack on 24 January by four US destroyers on the Japanese invasion fleet on their way to the island of Balikipapan, off the coast of Borneo. The US ships had total surprise on their side and managed to sink four of the Japanese transport ships before escaping unscathed. In early February a newly formed Allied Fleet under the command of Dutch Rear Admiral Doorman had tried to stop the Japanese invasion of Makassar but had failed. On the 13th a Dutch naval force had tried to intercept the Japanese forces landing at Palembang on the island of Sumatra without success. Six days later Allied ships clashed with the Japanese in the Lombok Straits and managed to damage a Imperial Navy destroyer and transport. They also suffered losses with a US and a Dutch cruiser being damaged during the running battle with the Japanese.

By late February most of the Netherlands East Indies had been conquered which only left the most important island, Java, in Allied hands. Doorman's fleet was now expected to do its utmost to stop the Japanese invasion of Java or at the very least inflict as much damage as possible in the attempt. The Allied Fleet had been put together using all available warships from the navies of Britain, the Netherlands, Australia and the USA. Most of the fleet were made up of Dutch ships with a handful of ships of the Royal Navy, Australian navy and US navy. On 26 February this multi-national fleet, under the command of Admiral Doorman, left the port of Surabaya in Sumatra to try and defeat the more modern and powerful Japanese fleet. Doorman's fleet was made up of two heavy cruisers, the USS *Houston* and the Royal Navy's HMS *Exeter*, and three light cruisers, the Dutch HNLMS *Java* and the HNLMS *De Ruyter*, which was the admiral's flagship, and the Australian HMAS *Perth*. The rest of the fleet included 9 destroyers (4 US, 3 Royal Navy and 2 Dutch). Although determined to put up a good fight, the 'cobbled together' fleet had several weaknesses. These included a breakdown in communication due to language differences and the varying types of battle command issued. They also did not have the 'long-lance' torpedo that the Imperial Navy was to use to such effect during the battle.

The Japanese fleet waiting for Doorman's doomed fleet had two groups, one under Admiral Kondo had 4 battleships, the *Kongo*, *Haruma*, *Hiei* and *Kurishima*, 3 heavy cruisers and 6 destroyers, whilst another force under under Admiral Nagumo had 4 carriers, 2 battleships and various escorting smaller ships. Nagumo's ships were stationed to stop any surviving Allied ship escaping from the scene after the inevitable defeat they faced. The battle was an 'unmitigated disaster' for the Allies with the

USS *Houston*, HMAS *Perth* and two of the Dutch cruisers, the HNLMS *Java* and HNLMS *De Ruyter*, being sunk. When HNLMS *De Ruyter* went down Admiral Doorman and his officers stayed at their posts until the end. By the end of the battle only HMS *Exeter* had survived but she was to be sunk along with her two escorting destroyers trying to escape through the Sunda Strait to the north-west of Java. Following the destruction of Doorman's fleet the Japanese invasion of Java could go on unopposed.

The Japanese navy's successes in the sea battles of early 1942 led its commanders to believe that their naval war should now be extended into the Indian Ocean. It was decided to launch a large-scale raid into the Bay of Bengal to attack the defences of the island of Ceylon. Ceylon, the British possession off the eastern coast of India, was vulnerable to attack and its conquest would put the Japanese navy in a strong position to stop Allied shipping moving anywhere in the Indian Ocean. Two Japanese fleets were assembled, one to attack Ceylon's coastal defences and the other to run amok in the Bay of Bengal. The Ceylon attack fleet was made up of 5 aircraft carriers with a total of 300 aircraft, 4 battleships, 2 heavy cruisers, 1 light cruiser and 8 destroyers. A smaller fleet to attack shipping in the Bay of Bengal had 1 light aircraft carrier, 6 cruisers and 8 destroyers.

Japanese navy plans for the operation caused consternation in the British war Cabinet, which worried that the Imperial Navy would now gain total air and naval superiority in the Indian Ocean. A powerful British Eastern Fleet was hastily assembled to counter the Japanese with three aircraft carriers, HMS *Indomitable*, HMS *Formidable* and the old 1919-era HMS *Hermes*. In addition there were 5 battleships, including HMS *Warspite*, 4 Sovereign class battleships, 2 heavy cruisers, 5 light cruisers, including a Dutch cruiser, 16 destroyers and 7 submarines, including 2 Dutch. Although the Eastern Fleet looked strong, its commander, Admiral Somerville, had vitally only 100 aged carrier aircraft to counter the Japanese 300 modern planes. During a series of engagements the Japanese navy sank a large number of merchant ships and Ceylon was attacked by ninety-one bombers and thirty-six fighters. On 9 April HMS *Hermes* was sunk along with the HMAS *Vampire*, an Australian destroyer. They had left the Singhalese port of Trincomalee and had been spotted by Japanese carrier planes and sunk within 10 minutes. Other Allied losses during the Japanese raid into the Indian Ocean were the two heavy cruisers HMS *Cornwall* and HMS *Dorsetshire*, both quickly sunk when they were attacked by fifty-three Japanese carrier planes. Although an invasion of Ceylon was not seriously considered by the Japanese, their raid into the Indian Ocean further affected the already low Allied morale. The war at sea was now to shift to the east of the recently occupied Netherlands East Indies into an area of the Pacific known as the Coral Sea. The Battle of the Coral Sea began on 1 May 1942 when the US navy found out about the Japanese plans to land troops on New Guinea and the Solomon Islands. A two-ship US carrier force made up of the USS *Lexington* and USS *Yorktown*, with escorting ships, set off from Pearl Harbor to intercept the Japanese landing force. The Japanese naval force escorting the invasion force was made up of the carriers *Shokaku* and *Zuikaku* and the light carrier *Shoho*, with an escorting fleet of another carrier and four heavy cruisers. When the US ships arrived at Tulagi on the night of 2–3 May the Japanese task force was not there but they did sink a number of enemy transport ships. When the two fleets did make contact the battle was to become an aerial conflict with neither side coming within gun range of each other. It was the carrier planes that were to fight each other and to inflict damage on each other's ships in an action controlled by radio. After seven days of aerial combat and attacks against each other's carriers the battle ended in what was described as a draw. The Japanese navy lost a destroyer and the *Shoho* was sunk by torpedo bombers from the two US carriers. US losses were a destroyer sunk and the USS *Lexington* so badly damaged it had to be scuttled. The *Shokaku* were also damaged and the *Zuikaku* lost a large number of its pilots in the battle. With the USS *Yorktown* having to limp back to Pearl Harbor for repairs, honours were pretty much even.

Although the seven-day battle was a keenly fought draw, it proved to be the 'high water mark' for the Japanese Imperial Navy. A month later the two fleets clashed again at the Battle of Midway in the Central Pacific and the balance was then to swing decisively in favour of the US navy.

The destroyer USS *William D. Preston* was the first US naval target after the attack on Pearl Harbor when she was bombed in the Gulf of Davao off the Philippines island of Mindanao. Attacked by thirteen Japanese dive-bombers on 8 December, she managed to escape having lost two of her three Catalina sea planes. Two days later a Japanese large-scale air raid took place on the US navy base at Cavite on Luzon in the Philippines. This raid saw the destruction of vital repair facilities and warehouses and the sinking of the submarine USS *Sealion* and the minelayer USS *Bittern*.

The HMS *Prince of Wales* was one of the best battleships in service with the Royal Navy in 1941. It had only been completed earlier in the year having been laid down in 1939 and was one of the KG V, or King George V, class battleships with a crew of 1,612. Her main armament of 10 14in guns and 16 5.25in guns was impressive and she was protected from air attack by 60 2-pounders. Unfortunately, with no carrier support this anti-aircraft armament would be of little use when she and HMS *Repulse*, known as Z Force, went into action. She is pictured leaving Singapore harbour to go on her doomed mission to attack the Japanese ships landing troops in northern Malaya.

HMS *Repulse* was an older ship than the *Prince of Wales* having been completed in 1916 and was designated as a battle-cruiser with a crew of 1,309. Battle-cruisers generally sacrificed the thickness of their deck armour to increase their speed which made them highly susceptible to air attack. *Repulse's* anti-aircraft guns were also not adequate as she only had eight 4in guns to defend her from Japanese attack. With slightly bigger guns than the *Prince of Wales*, the *Repulse* was still a potent war ship but had little chance to prove this in December 1941. Z Force was made up of the two battleships and four escort destroyers; the aircraft carrier HMS *Indomitable* was still in port in Jamaica when battle was joined.

This Japanese navy photograph shows the view from a reconnaissance plane of the HMS *Prince of Wales* and HMS *Repulse* under attack. Both ships try desperately to take evasive action as bombs fall around them but it was the torpedo bombers that did the most damage. The one-sided battle began at 11.00 am on 10 December, the first attacks coming from high-level bombers. About 30 minutes later the first torpedo attacks began, two torpedoes hitting the *Prince of Wales*. Further bombing and torpedo attacks continued at 12.22 pm and another three torpedoes hit the *Prince of Wales*. The bombers then concentrated on the *Repulse*, which was hit five times sinking only 11 minutes later. At 12.46 pm the final attacks on the *Prince of Wales* came from bombers which penetrated the main deck sinking the battleship at 13.20 pm.

Crew members desperately try to scramble from the deck of the sinking HMS *Prince of Wales* to a rescue ship. The *Prince of Wales* and the *Repulse* had been bombed and hit by three torpedoes from Japanese aircraft flying from Saigon in French Indo-China. Air cover was supposed to be provided by RAF planes taking off from their airfields in northern Malaya. These airfields had already largely fallen to Japanese attack but the mission still went ahead. Both ships were sunk within an hour of each other with 796 men of the *Repulse* rescued and 1,285 of the *Prince of Wales* crew saved. The sinking of these two great battleships cost the Japanese only three downed aircraft and their crews.

A fly past of two different outdated types of floatplane takes place in 1941 in the Netherlands East Indies. The large, ungainly planes are Dutch-made Fokker T.IVA bomber-reconnaissance planes which first flew in 1927. All of these planes were destroyed by the Netherlands East Indies navy before the fighting began. In the foreground are three US-made Ryan PT-20 trainers with floats added which may have seen limited service as liaison planes in 1942.

Japanese Imperial Navy battleships act as escorts for the invasion of the Philippines as one prepares to launch its reconnaissance seaplane to search for the weakened Allied fleets. After the events at Pearl Harbor the Japanese fleet in the Pacific had free reign as the US navy and Royal Navy tried to recover. Even during this period of superiority the Imperial Navy's command realized that in the long-term the odds would be stacked against them. One of the Japanese navy's main weaknesses was its lack of cruisers which were essential to hold onto the empire's much extended naval perimeter.

The two-man crew of a Japanese navy Nakajima E8NI reconnaissance floatplane connect the hook of the crane which will hoist their plane into the Pacific Ocean. Japanese Imperial Navy seaplanes launched from warships searched the ocean for the merchant and naval ships of the various Allied navies. Without the air cover that aircraft carriers would have provided, the British, Dutch, Australian and US navies were at a great disadvantage in 1941–2.

The Burmese crew of a shore gun prepare to fire it in the early stages of the land campaign for Burma in early 1942. This gun is part of the poorly organized coastal defences on the northern shores of the Bay of Bengal off the southern coast of Burma. Once the south of Burma had fallen to the Imperial Army, the Japanese navy would have free reign in the Indian Ocean. This would leave the east coast of India and the island of Ceylon open to naval attacks by the Japanese Imperial Fleet.

Laid down in 1925, the HNLMS *Kortenaer* was a Admiralen class destroyer armed with 4 4.7in guns, 2 3in guns and 6 21in torpedo tubes. She took part in the ill-fated Battle of the Java Sea and was torpedoed by the Imperial Navy's cruiser the *Haguro*. When she sank 113 of her 153-man crew were rescued by HMS *Encounter*, which took them to the port of Surabaya on Java. Their respite was to be short, however, as Java was invaded by the Japanese a few days after the naval battle had ended.

The light cruiser HNLMS *De Ruyter* was the flag ship of the Dutch Admiral Doorman during the Battle of the Java Sea. She was a unique one-off design which began life as a lightly armed ship due to the economic and political restrictions of the 1930s in the Netherlands. Every effort had been made during her design and construction to cut costs in the depression-hit Netherlands. She joined two other cruisers in the defence of the Netherlands East Indies and was damaged in actions on 4 and 18 February 1942.

The HNLMS *De Ruyter* fires a broadside from its seven 5.9in guns during sea manoeuvres before the outbreak of the war with Japan. Doorman's fleet of 2 heavy cruisers, 2 light cruisers and 9 destroyers tried to attack the Japanese invasion fleet on its way to Java on 26 February. They encountered a similar sized Japanese fleet of 2 heavy cruisers, 2 light cruisers and 14 destroyers. His mixed force of Dutch, British, Australian and American ships had communication problems and the fleet was disorganized. They were faced also by the Japanese Imperial Navy's secret weapon the 'long-lance' torpedo, which accounted for several of Doorman's ships.

Two double-barrelled 40mm anti-aircraft guns on the Dutch light cruiser HMLMS *De Ruyter* are seen on a raised platform on the ship's rear deck. Launched in 1935, the *De Ruyter* had ten of these 40mm Bofors guns but most were situated on the one platform. She also had 8 0.5in Browning machine guns to supplement the Bofors and two Fokker C-11W floatplanes on her decks. The *De Ruyter* was sunk by a single torpedo at 2.30 am on 28 February having been hit 3 hours earlier and 345 men went down with her. Admiral Doorman and the ship's captain Lacomble in time-honoured tradition both went down with their vessel.

A Dutch post-war recruiting poster celebrates the heroism of Admiral Doorman, the commander of the combined ABDA fleet in 1942. There was no doubting the bravery of Doorman and the captains of his ships during the Battle of the Java Sea. The poster says: 'I attack ... Follow me' and addressing the Dutch youth of 1947 it goes on to say, 'This message also applies to you'.

IK VAL AAN...
VOLGT MIJ
DIT SEIN
waarmee schout-bij-nacht Doorman
de Japansche vloot tegemoet ging in 1942
GELDT OOK VOOR U

The heavy cruiser HMS *Exeter* is seen at sea in the days before the ill-fated Battle of the Java Sea when she formed part of Admiral Doorman's fleet. She had won fame during the 1939 Battle of the River Plate which led to the scuttling of the German pocket battleship *Graf Spee*. Launched in 1929, the *Exeter* had six 8in guns and put up a great fight during her last battle as she tried to slip through the Sunda Strait. She had been damaged in the Java Sea action and was trying to evade the Japanese ships along with two British destroyers.

The heavy cruiser USS *Houston* was another of the ships in Doorman's fleet that fought in the Battle of the Java Sea. Although the *Houston* survived the battle, she was sunk after attacking an invasion force landing at Bantam Bay in Java on 28 February. With only four 8in guns left in action after being damaged in an earlier sea battle near Timor, she was faced with Japanese heavy cruisers each with ten guns of a similar calibre. During the battle the *Houston* and an Australian ship, HMAS *Perth*, accounted for a Japanese minesweeper and four transport ships as well as damaging three destroyers. Both Allied ships were eventually sunk with the *Houston* losing 65 per cent of her crew, including Captain Albert Rooks.

The Australian cruiser HMAS *Perth* survived the Battle of the Java Sea in late February 1942 but was sunk on 1 March during the Battle of the Sunda Strait. She went down with the USS *Houston* as they tried to get through the stretch of water between Java and Sumatra. Their captains had been told that the strait was free of Japanese ships but this intelligence was incorrect and the *Perth* was soon surrounded by Imperial Navy ships. She was hit by four torpedoes within a few minutes and sank at 12.25 am, only 20 minutes after being hit. Out of her 646 crew, 353 were killed when she sank and another 106 were to die as prisoners of war in Japanese camps before 1945.

B-25 Mitchell bombers are lined up 'toe to toe' on the flight deck of the USS *Hornet* while sailing towards Japan. The sixteen Mitchells were under the command of Lieutenant Colonel J.H. Doolittle and his plan was to bomb Tokyo and several other Japanese cities. On 18 April 1942 they took off from the *Hornet*, which was 750 miles from their target. They were escorted by fighters from the USS *Enterprise* for their bombing raid, which was a major propaganda coup for the USA. As well as Tokyo, the bombers hit four other cities causing consternation and outrage amongst the Japanese public. Unable to land back on the carrier, most managed to reach China whilst two got to Siberia. Several crashed in Japanese-occupied China and some of their crew members were executed in October in retaliation for this 'outrage'.

A gunboat of the Indian navy is crewed by volunteers of the Ceylon Royal Navy Volunteers Reserves. The threat of a Japanese invasion of Ceylon led, according to the caption to this photograph, to a 'valiant response' from the Singhalese population. This gunboat is patrolling the waters around the island which came under attack from the Imperial Navy in April 1942.

Japanese Imperial Navy ships sail into the Indian Ocean on 30 March 1942 to cause as much havoc as possible. There were five battleships in the Japanese fleet that undertook this large-scale raid and they are seen here in a line and include the ship in the foreground. The Indian Ocean raid was a success for the Japanese with Royal Navy losses totalling 1 light carrier, 2 heavy cruisers, 1 armed merchant cruiser and a corvette and a sloop. In addition, twenty-three merchant ships were sunk by the Japanese and forty aircraft were also destroyed. On the Japanese side the main losses were in aircraft and their irreplaceable crew with an estimated twenty being shot down during the raid.

The Japanese battleship *Haruna* is seen taking part in the Imperial Navy's Indian Ocean raid in April 1942. Launched in 1913, the *Haruna* had been updated during the 1930s and had an armament of 8 14in guns, 16 6in guns and 12 5in guns. It was one of its three Jake floatplanes that spotted the Royal Navy aircraft carrier HMS *Hermes* during the raid. The *Hermes* was sunk after being hit by forty bombs dropped by planes from three Pearl Harbor veteran aircraft carriers, the *Akagi, Soryu and Hiryu*.

The British destroyer HMS *Cornwall* on fire and about to sink after being heavily attacked by the Japanese fleet which had moved into the Indian Ocean in April 1942. This large-scale raid by the Japanese navy was intended to cause as much havoc as possible and threaten Ceylon. Japanese ships sank 135,000 tons of Allied shipping during their foray into the Bay of Bengal. Most of the transports had been shipping troops and supplies to the beleaguered defenders of Burma.

HMS *Paladin*, a P class destroyer, was launched in July 1940 and had been transferred to the British Eastern Fleet in June 1941. She was on station in the Indian Ocean when the Japanese made their raid towards Ceylon in April 1942. On 5 April the *Paladin*'s crew was able to rescue 1,120 crewmen from the two destroyers HMS *Cornwall* and HMS *Dorsetshire*, which had been sunk by Japanese ships. The desperate survivors of the *Cornwall* had clung to life in shark-infested waters for 30 hours.

The US navy fleet carrier the USS *Yorktown* sails through the South Pacific towards the Solomon Islands. Although the *Yorktown* was to survive the Battle of the Coral Sea in early May 1942, it was damaged and had to go to port for repairs. During the battle aircraft from the *Yorktown* and USS *Lexington* were able to sink a Japanese light carrier, the *Shoho*. Other Japanese losses included a destroyer and three smaller warships sunk, whilst the fleet carrier *Shokaku*, a destroyer, a transport and a smaller ship were damaged.

The planes of the Japanese fleet carrier *Zuikaku* prepare to take off to attack their prime targets, the US carriers USS *Lexington* and USS *Yorktown*. During the war at sea in the Pacific the sinking of enemy aircraft carriers became the greatest prize. Both the Japanese and US fleets were now judged by the number of carriers they had as their battleships became less and less effective. The sinking of the British navy's battleships off the coast of Malaya had proved that these ships were no longer viable without the air cover provided by carriers.

The USS *Lexington*, known affectionately as the 'Lady Lex', lists dangerously after she was hit by aerial torpedoes at 11.27 am on 8 May during the Battle of the Coral Sea. Many of her crew jumped into the sea from the flight deck without having received orders to abandon ship. When aircraft returned from their attacks on the Japanese fleet they were unable to land on the damaged deck. Hours later the abandoned *Lexington* was sunk by a US torpedo in order to stop the carrier falling into Japanese hands.

The Japanese Imperial Navy's fleet carrier the *Shokaku*, which was damaged during the Battle of the Coral Sea on 8 May. Here she is seen making a sharp turn in an attempt to avoid planes from US navy carriers attacking her. Both sides suffered heavy losses in aircraft as well as ships during the battle which lasted from 1–8 May. The US navy lost a total of sixty-nine aircraft whilst the Imperial Navy suffered heavier losses with ninety-two aircraft destroyed.

Chapter Thirteen

The Conquest of the Netherlands East Indies, 1942

With Malaya and Singapore conquered and the Philippines virtually under their control, the Japanese Imperial Army could now concentrate on the main prize, the Netherlands East Indies. The Netherlands East Indies' oilfields on the islands of Borneo, Java and Sumatra were vital to Japan's plans. Although these oilfields produced only 2.8 per cent of the world's crude oil, this would be adequate to fuel the Japanese economy and war effort. The Netherlands East Indies Army, or KNIL, however, could not hope to defend even a minority of the 17,500 islands which made up the East Indies. It had to spread its meagre resources to the most strategically important islands such as Java, Sumatra, Celebes and Borneo. When the fighting in the Netherlands East Indies began the KNIL was distributed as follows. On the most important island, Java, there were about 50,000 troops, regular and irregular, and on Sumatra there were 8,500. Other smaller garrisons included 6,600 in Dutch Borneo, 1,300 in Dutch New Guinea and 2,300 on the island of Celebes. Scattered amongst the many islands to the east of Java were a paltry 500 troops who manned the token garrisons guarding them.

The Japanese invasion forces for the Netherlands East Indies were divided into Western, Central and Eastern forces. The Western Force was to be concentrated at Camranh Bay in Vietnam and its targets were southern Sumatra, Banka and the Sumatran city of Palembang. Once these objectives had been reached the force would move to western Java. The Central Force was to set out from Davao in the Philippines and attack Tarakan, Balikpapan, Bandjormasin and then eastern Java. The Eastern Force was again to set out from Davao and its objectives were the outlying islands of Manado, Kendora, Ambon, Makassar, Timor and Bali. In January 1942 the two oil-producing islands of Tarakan and Balikpapan fell to the Japanese with both defended by small garrisons. Tarakan, which fell in early January, was defended by the 7th KNIL Infantry Battalion, a machine-gun company and some coastal and anti-aircraft guns as well as seven armoured cars. Balikpapan was garrisoned by 1,100 KNIL troops and was fought over between 23 and 24 January. Between 23 of January and 9 February the Japanese took the islands of Ambon and Kendari as well as the port of Makassar. Sumatra was invaded on 16 February with the strategic east of the island soon falling to Japanese ground and airborne forces.

As the 7,000 or so KNIL ground forces surrendered to the Japanese any remaining Dutch and British aircraft were sent to Java to help in that island's defence. On the 19th the island of Bali was invaded leaving only Java unconquered and any chance of it being defended would be decided in the naval Battle of the Java Sea in late February (see Chapter Twelve). The defeat of the composite Allied navy during the battle sealed the fate of Java where the defenders awaited the Japanese with trepidation. Java was defended by 25,000 regulars of the KNIL and 40,000 of the second-line Stadwacht, who were poorly trained and armed. The vast majority of the KNIL personnel were as usual native troops whose loyalty the Dutch regarded with increasing suspicion.

Besides the KNIL troops, the defence of Java could also call on contingents from the British, Australian and US armies. There was a 5,500-strong British force made up a mixture of various second-line troops and redundant artillerymen evacuated from Singapore. The 3,000 Australians known as 'Black Force' were under the command of Brigadier Blackburn. They were made up of a mish-mash of battalions and companies. US troops in Java were all artillerymen and included 750 men from the 26th Field Artillery Brigade and the 131st Field Artillery Regiment, which was part of the Texas National Guard. In February the Allies were 'strengthened' by 12,000 British soldiers, mostly support troops who had escaped from Singapore. They had little equipment and were not trained for front-line combat roles and included RAF ground crews and the crews of heavy anti-aircraft guns.

The Japanese 16th Army landed in the far west and north of Java on 28 February and quickly advanced towards their various objectives. Batavia, the administrative capital of Java, fell on 2 March while the port of Surabaya in the east of the island fell on 7 March. During the first week in March the chaotic defences only slightly delayed the Japanese advance and the Dutch government withdrew to the mountain city of Bandeong. It was not that the Dutch and their Allies were not fighting bravely, but they were totally disorganized and small units were defending their own sectors. With little co-ordination between the various units the Japanese were able to pick them off piecemeal and resistance now became futile. There was little choice for the Dutch leadership but to surrender, which they did on 7 March. Any surviving Allied soldiers were marched off to imprisonment from which many of them were not to return to their homelands.

A machine-gun section of the KNIL poses for the news camera at the start of the 1941–2 campaign. The NCO looks for targets for his team whilst the loader armed with a carbine and the machine-gunner prepare fire. Danish-designed Madsen light machine guns were the main type in service with the KNIL during the fighting. This widely used model, the M25 Karabijn Mitrailleur, has the shortened barrel which was popular with the soldiers because it was lighter and easier to carry than the standard type. First produced in 1908, the Madsen was reliable and was pressed into service with the Japanese after 1942.

Marines of the Netherlands East Indies navy are about to disembark on to one of the hundreds of islands that made up the Indonesian archipelago in early 1941. Just like the KNIL, the navy and its marine units had Dutch officers and NCOs and native other ranks. These marines wear their distinctive slouch hats, issued in straw or canvas, with the name of their ship in white on a black band. In combat their hats would hopefully be replaced with the Model 1928 Dutch helmet.

A Fokker C.X. light bomber sits on the airfield in the build up to the Japanese invasion of the Netherlands East Indies. The C.X. was designed in 1933 and came into ML-KNIL service in 1936 to replace the C.V. planes but was out of date by 1941–2. All 13 delivered to the ML-KNIL were used for training and liaison work up until the Japanese invasion. Although the C.X. had proved to be an adequate anti-insurgency plane in the 1930s, it was totally outclassed by its Japanese opponents in 1942.

Pilots and ground crew of the KNIL (ML-KNIL) line up in front of their US-made Curtiss-Wright 21B fighters. They belong to the 2-VLG-IV Squadron which flew this type of fighter, which had been rejected by the US air force. The CW-21 was a fast and lightweight plane which was offered to several nations including Nationalist China. It was initially ordered by the Dutch government in 1940 but the fall of the Netherlands led to this order being transferred to the Netherlands East Indies. By the time the fighting began the number of CW-21Bs available was down from twenty-five to fifteen aircraft. These fought bravely against the Japanese scoring several victories including at least one against the dreaded Zero.

These Kawasaki KI-45 KAI-Otsu fighters belong to the 1st Chutai of the 21st Sentai which had previously seen action in Burma and Malaya. The unit moved on to fight during the conquest of the Netherlands East Indies with their 20mm Ho-3 nose cannon devastating the opposition. KI-45s, which were described as 'strategic fighters', were quite advanced for the time and were to go on to serve in the Imperial Army air arm until August 1945.

Hawk 75A-7s of the ML-KNIL fly in formation over the main island of Java. These US-made fighters were to take part in what was described as a 'brief but vicious action' on 19 February in which the Allies lost seventy-five of their precious planes. Although the Allies and their aircraft were outclassed in 1942 by the Japanese, there was certainly no lack of bravery on the part of their pilots.

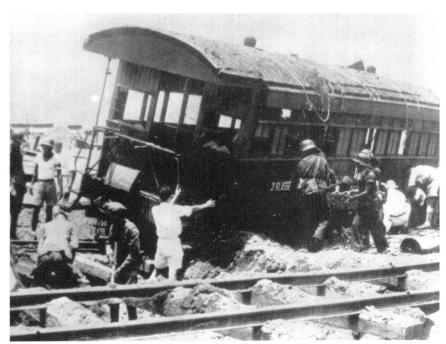

Air-raid wardens in Surabaya on the island of Java try to dig out a railway carriage which has been damaged during a Japanese raid in February 1942. The civil defence forces in Java were largely manned by Indonesians with some units given rifles. Interestingly, some of the personnel were issued with copies of the German M35 steel helmet made in a local factory by the Braat company. Although the detail in this photograph is not too clear, you can see that several of the volunteers in it are wearing the Braat helmet.

Reservists of the KNIL move through the centre of a town on the main Indonesian island of Java. The age of these men shows the type of volunteer who served in the Stadwacht and other auxiliary forces. Their uniform is the same as the KNIL regulars but usually they wore a tin badge on the left breast. This often featured the name of the city they served in embossed on the front over the word 'Stadwacht', or city watch.

The crew of a Kanon van 4.7cm anti-tank gun rides to its position on a Vickers utility tractor. Equipment used by the KNIL came from a wide variety of sources. In this case the anti-tank gun was bought from Austria, where it was manufactured as the 4.7 Bohler. Their artillery tractor was produced in Belgium and used to tow their anti-tank guns and was adopted by the Dutch before 1940.

The lack of resources in the Netherlands East Indies led to the building of several improvised military vehicles such as this one built around a Chevrolet civilian truck. A flat bed has been added and a 12.7mm Colt-Browning M.30 machine gun mounted on its back. Anti-aircraft trucks like this were made in various workshops in the build up to the 1942 campaign. As the loader looks to the sky for signs of Japanese aircraft, the gunner is cradled in a canvas sling and steadies his feet against the metal stanchion.

Some of the 700 oil wells on the island of Tarakan, which was part of Dutch Borneo. Not surprisingly, the Japanese saw the island's oil wells and also its refinery and air field as great prizes. Their plan was to invade using the Sakaguchi Detachment, which had been formed from units of the 56th Infantry Division. They would be reinforced by a battalion-strong 'Kure' Naval Landing Force of the Imperial Navy. The dense jungles of Borneo were a much tougher proposition than those in Malaya but the Japanese were used to dealing with this kind of terrain.

Soldiers of the KNIL prepare to make a night crossing from the island of Celebes to reinforce their forces at Tarakan in Dutch Borneo in January 1942. They are wearing their issue overcoats and green rattan hats and most appear also to have steel helmets with canvas covers on. The machine-gunner is armed with the Dutch version of the Lewis light machine gun, the M20. KNIL machine-gunners had three main models of light machine gun, the Madsen, the Lewis and the Colt R75 heavy automatic rifle.

A 81mm mortar crew of the KNIL on Tarakan prepare for the expected Japanese invasion of the oil-rich island. They are part of the 1,300-strong garrison which tried in vain to defend the island when it was invaded on 10 January 1942. When Tarakan fell 219 of the garrison were murdered by the Japanese by drowning in revenge for their stubborn resistance.

Japanese naval landing forces move cautiously towards a village on the outskirts of a village on Tarakan Island in Dutch Borneo in January 1942. The naval landing forces were an equivalent to the US marines and were initially formed as ad-hoc ground forces taken from the crews of navy ships. As the infantry force of the Imperial Navy they had to be greatly expanded during 1941–2 to fulfil the navy's infantry role in several land campaigns. This meant that the ranks were stocked with raw recruits and unwanted troops transferred from other units. Because of the rapid expansion the naval landing force's reputation as a well-trained arm suffered.

In a rare action photograph from January 1942 KNIL soldiers rush to man their positions during a threatened Japanese attack on the island of Tarakan. Tarakan was a large island of 177 square miles and its garrison was totally inadequate having only 1,300 men. They were supported by 8 75mm field guns, a few anti-aircraft guns and seven armoured cars.

KNIL artillerymen assemble their mountain gun in a jungle clearing on the island of Java in 1942. Although all the main islands of the Netherlands East Indies were garrisoned to some degree, Java had the majority of troops, 50,000 in total. Java was always seen by the Dutch colonial authorities as by far the most important island in the Netherlands East Indies and it had the largest population and was home to the administrative capital at Batavia. KNIL troops were assisted in their defence of the island by small forces made up of British, Australian and US troops who had largely been evacuated from Malaya before the fall of Singapore.

Japanese naval landing troops march under the Rising Sun flag at Kendari on the recently conquered Netherlands East Indies island of Celebes. The Japanese conquest of Celebes was in two stages and Kendari in the east fell on 24 January. Japanese forces then took the west of the island and its main city Makassar on 8 February.

These parachutists are about to be dropped over the city of Palembang on the island of Sumatra on 14 February 1942. During the conquest of the Netherlands East Indies there were a number of parachute drops by the Japanese with varying success. In February 334 paratroopers jumped over the island of Celebes but were too high when they left the plane and ended up scattered for miles. Another 350-strong unit dropped on the island of Timor in mid-February in support of the 228th Infantry Regiment and naval landing forces. The idea of using airborne troops had not even been discussed until September 1940 and by December that year the first 200 paratroops were training in the puppet state of Manchukuo.

This romanticized Japanese propaganda painting shows the landing of the parachute force on the airfield at Palembang at 11.26 am on 14 February. During the initial assault the paratroopers are having to fight off the KNIL defenders armed only with their Nambu automatic pistols and grenades. Whilst they do this, their comrades are opening up their metal canisters containing the carbines, sub-machine guns, machine guns and light mortars. As they secured the air field, their comrades were landing further north on the Sumatran coast.

A Japanese transport ship sails towards Palembang in southern Sumatra where burning oilfields light up the sky. The Japanese paratrooper force that captured Palembang airfield suffered heavy losses during the assault. This initial setback meant that their orders to move on to take the oilfields close to the city were fatally delayed. Dutch defenders were then able to blow up the oilfields and storage tanks which had been an important target for the Japanese.

A group of KNIL troops in Java who have just returned from fighting for the city of Palembang on Sumatra, 20 February 1942. The men in the photograph are a real mixture of ethnicities with the men in the front coming from the islands of Java, Ambon and northern Celebes. Behind stand two other soldiers, one a mixed race Indo-European and the other a Dutch soldier. Although they are being sent to defend Batavia, it was declared an open city on 1 March. Five days later the Japanese, having been informed of Batavia's status, entered the city to complete their conquest.

Japanese cycle troops ride into the centre of Batavia on 6 March as the Imperial Army continued to use their 'secret weapon'. The 2nd Imperial Division that took Batavia, like every Japanese infantry division, would have been issued with 6,000 bicycles. During the various campaigns of the 1941–2 offensive some Japanese troops were known to cycle up to 20 hours a day! According to intelligence reports, many of them could not walk a step after spending so much time on their bicycles.

Japanese soldiers stand on a jungle road on some unidentified Netherlands East Indies island in spring 1942. By this time most of the Netherlands East Indies had fallen and it was only a matter of mopping up the outlying islands, mainly to the east of Java. Some of the islands would never be occupied as the Japanese Imperial Army and Navy had to ration their limited resources. If they did land on one of the smaller or more remote islands they were not going to be faced with much opposition. It was estimated that all of the many islands to the East of Java had a total of 500 KNIL regulars and a few home guardsmen to defend them.

Imperial Army soldiers perform the obligatory Banzai in front of a captured KNIL Braat armoured vehicle. The armoured car has been quickly adorned with the Japanese flag to show its new ownership. Because of the shortages of Japanese KNIL equipment, vehicles and weapons captured by the Imperial Army were immediately pressed into Japanese service.

The two top Dutch civil and military leaders of the Netherlands East Indies are escorted by their Japanese captors into a prison camp at the end of the fighting. They are Lieutenant General Hein Te Poorten, the commander in chief of all Dutch forces in the East Indies, and Alidius Tjarda van Starkenburgh Stachouwer, the governor general. Both men were concerned about the fate of the Dutch residents of Java, many of whom lived amongst a hostile Indonesian population. On 8 March the Dutch surrendered leaving their British, Australian and US allies on Java with little choice but to retreat.

Chapter Fourteen

Japan's Spreading Tentacles, 1941-2

Away from the main theatres of war in South-East Asia and the Pacific the victorious Japanese war machine continued its conquests from December 1941 until mid-1942. Whilst the Japanese Imperial Army, Navy and Air Forces had been advancing through Malaya, the Philippines, Burma and the Netherlands East Indies, smaller offensive operations were taking place elsewhere. These widespread actions were illustrated in some propaganda cartoons in the form of a menacing red octopus. The body of the octopus was the Japanese home islands and its tentacles reached out to the east and south. They spread eastwards into the vast Pacific Ocean and south-eastwards into the South Pacific, whilst its other tentacles reached northwards into Korea and China from the late 1800s and on into the 1930s.

Although the large island of Borneo was regarded as part of the conquest of the East Indies, it was really a 'sideshow' of that campaign. The conquest of Borneo, which was divided between British territories and the Dutch, took place in two stages. British-controlled Borneo fell between December 1941 and January 1942. When the Japanese conquered the Netherlands East Indies the remainder of the vast island, known as Dutch Guinea was taken by February 1942. Timor to the east of the Netherlands East Indies was divided between neutral Portugal and the Dutch and had been invaded by a mixed Dutch-Australian force, 'Sparrow Force', in December 1941. The Japanese were willing to acknowledge Portuguese neutrality but still took over the whole of Timor after invading on 20 February 1942. They faced continued resistance from Sparrow Force for several months before the guerrilla force was evacuated by sea.

In February 1942 the Japanese also launched several air raids on the northern Australian port and city of Darwin. The large-scale raids were seen by some as a precursor to a full-blown invasion of northern Australia but this was never in the Japanese war plans. As far as the Japanese were concerned, the raids on Darwin were simply to try and disrupt the supply routes to the next target of Japanese aggression, Australian-controlled New Guinea.

In March 1942 the Japanese occupied the British possessions of the Nicobar and Andaman islands in the Indian Ocean to the west of Burma. The islands were taken on 25 March, almost two weeks after their garrison had been evacuated. Up to January

1942 the garrison had been made up 300 Sikh militia led by a handful of British officers. A detachment of the 4/12th Frontier Force Regiment of the 16th Indian Brigade had been sent to the Andamans as reinforcement. It was realized that the garrison was too small to put up much of a fight against the expected Japanese invasion so it was removed. The Japanese had also taken two islands in the Aleutian Island chain in the Eastern Pacific which was only 900 miles away from the US territory of Alaska. Their landings on the islands of Attu and Kiska in June 1942 were deemed to be a waste of time and resources after the defeat of the Japanese Imperial Navy at Midway the same month. Midway was the turning point of the war in the Pacific and after June 1942 the Japanese were increasingly on the defensive at sea and on land. One of the last invasions by Japanese forces in the Second World War saw the occupation of three small islands, Aru, Tanimbar and Kei between Timor and New Guinea, in July 1942.

From early 1942 the Japanese Imperial High Command had been looking for options in continuing their conquests in the Pacific. It was suggested that an invasion of India from Burma would be a possibility, as would an invasion of Ceylon. Other advisors suggested cutting off Australia from its allies by taking Fiji, New Caledonia and Samoa. This would mean that Australia would be isolated and although not conquered would be impotent in the war in the Pacific. The invasion of New Guinea in April 1942 and the Solomon Islands in May 1942 was to be a step too far for Japan. These actions were to embroil the Japanese in campaigns that their dwindling resources could not support. From May–June 1942 onwards the Japanese offensive in the Pacific was ended and a three-year period of defensive warfare ensued.

This painting by a Japanese war artist shows troops climbing into their landing craft during the invasion of northern Borneo in December 1941. The conquest of British Borneo was a drawn-out affair with the first Japanese soldiers landing on 15 December and taking the towns of Miri and Kuching in the north. Other parts of the large island did not fall until January and February 1942 and the largest town in Dutch Borneo not until 10 February. Most the interior of this jungle-covered island was left untouched by the Japanese who could not spare the troops to conquer empty wasteland.

Japanese soldiers prepare to embark on a civilian steamer during one of the many operations to capture Pacific Islands in 1941–2. During the offensive period it was relatively easy to capture poorly defended islands and establish garrisons on them. However, keeping these often isolated garrisons supplied from late 1942 proved almost impossible. As the US navy established superiority in the Pacific, these garrisons were often left to fend for themselves.

Japanese naval landing forces move through the town of Kavieng on the island of New Ireland on 23 January 1942. New Ireland was virtually undefended, as was the nearby island of New Britain, where the main settlement, Rabaul, was also taken on the same day. Fighting to take back control of these islands, which formed part of the Bismarck Archipelago, was to begin in a little over a year's time from when they were captured by the Japanese.

Japanese medium bombers are seen en route to the northern Australian port of Darwin which was heavily bombed in mid-February 1942. The destruction caused in Darwin sent shock waves through the Australian population who genuinely feared a Japanese invasion. In reality, the Japanese Imperial Army and Navy were already totally overstretched without trying to invade even part of Australia. Any invasion would have been heavily resisted by regular and irregular Australian forces. They would have used Australia's vast terrain to their advantage to fight a guerrilla war and the Japanese must have been aware of the difficulties they would face. (Cody Images)

The crew of an Australian 3.7in anti-aircraft gun fires at Japanese aircraft attacking the city of Darwin in northern Australia. Japan wanted to destroy as much of Darwin's port facilities as possible and launched 188 planes against them in 2 separate raids on 19 February 1942. With only a few US P-40 fighters available for the defence of the city, the Japanese bombers encountered little opposition. The only Australian planes in the vicinity were five Wirraway trainers which had been grounded for repairs. During the 2 raids the Japanese sank 8 ships and destroyed 24 aircraft as well as killing 250 people and wounding a further 320. The expected Japanese invasion of northern Australia did not materialize but the air raids heightened the awareness of the Australian population that the war was not very far away.

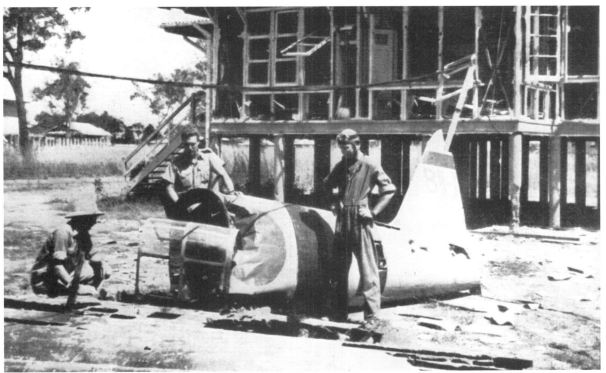

An Australian pilot and two ground crew examine the wreckage of a A6M Zero fighter shot down during the attack on the port of Darwin in February 1942. The Australian government was genuinely worried that a Japanese invasion of northern Australia could be a possibility. They moved 14,000 men into the Darwin area in March with another 10,000 following later. The USA also sent 6,000 troops to the region and the air defences were increased with 3 squadrons of fighters included 1 of American P-40M Kittyhawks. In reality, the Japanese had no plans to invade Australia but their victories in 1941–2 meant that their enemies believed that an invasion was a credible threat.

Japanese naval landing force troops gather together on the deck of their landing craft before going ashore on yet another Pacific island. The success of the Japanese Imperial Army and Navy caused what has been described as 'victory disease'. Their largely unexpected successes in 1941–2 meant that the Japanese outreached themselves in the Pacific and overextended their supply lines. Whilst small garrisons could easily hold their respective Pacific Islands in 1942 and 1943, they were often isolated with little support from their command.

Japanese naval landing troops celebrate the fall of Christmas Island on 1 April 1942. The island was a British possession 185 miles to the south of Java and was garrisoned by thirty-two Indian artillerymen with British officers. On 11 March the Indian troops mutinied and murdered five British officers throwing their bodies into the sea. The Japanese took over the island and its precious phosphate deposits 20 days later with 850 naval landing troops. Here the victorious Japanese stand on the island's main defence, its 1900 model 150mm gun, which had been emplaced there in 1940.

A recently captured anti-aircraft gunner of the British Indian Army is seen on the cover of a Japanese propaganda magazine in March 1942. He is one of the gunners who was 'persuaded' by the Japanese to be transported with their Bofors anti-aircraft guns to man them on a few of the Pacific Islands. At the time the Japanese were desperately short of anti-aircraft guns and these well-trained 'volunteers' were amongst the first to fight for them. This man's new allegiance is indicated by the small rising sun flag patch above the right breast pocket of his British khaki drill uniform.

寫眞週報

情報局編輯

Australian fighters of the guerrilla force known as Sparrow Force are seen in a rare photograph on the island of Timor attacking the Japanese occupiers. The Japanese had invaded on 20 February 1942 but Allied guerrillas attacked them for several months. These men made up a guerrilla army along with Dutch soldiers who had jointly defended the island from Japanese invasion since December 1941. The situation in Timor was complicated by the presence of neutral Portuguese troops as the island had been divided between Portugal and the Netherlands.

A US air force B-17 Flying Fortress prepares to take off from its Hawaiian base for a bombing raid on the Japanese in April 1942. Any surviving B-17 bombers in the Pacific had to be used sparingly until reinforcements could arrive from the USA. In early April, however, a force of thirteen US bombers was personally led by Brigadier General Ralph Royce from Australia back to the Philippines. This ad-hoc force was made up of three B-17s and ten B-25 Mitchell bombers and set up its temporary bases in unoccupied parts of the island of Mindanao. For a few days the bombers attacked Japanese targets on the Philippines islands of Cebu, Luzon and Davao. Having lost a number of planes during these attacks, which were meant to relieve the pressure on the besieged garrison on Corriegidor, the survivors flew back to Australia on 13 April.

A 25-pounder field gun of the Australian army is emplaced in a gun position on the Pacific island of Nauru in 1942. This tiny island, administered by the Australians and with a population of just 1,500 people, was coveted by the Japanese because of its phosphate deposits. An abortive attempt was made by the Japanese to invade in May 1942 but they successfully landed a few hundred men on 29 August. By that time the small garrison and some civilians had been evacuated leaving behind the native population and some Chinese labourers. They were to suffer terribly during the three-year occupation by the Imperial Navy who executed some and deported others to different islands.

Japanese naval landing troops stand outside their barracks on one of the more remote of the Philippines islands in 1942. The Philippines are made up of several large islands such as Luzon and Mindanao and many smaller islands. Some of these islands would have been garrisoned whilst others would not depending on their population or strategic importance. Garrison duty for the Japanese was often tedious, although a rising guerrilla movement in some areas meant that these Japanese special naval landing forces would have had to be on the alert.

The cover of one of the many illustrated propaganda magazines produced by the Japanese features three naval landing force troops enjoying the 'fruits of victory'. The euphoria felt by the Japanese Imperial Army in the aftermath of their victory over the Allied forces was often short-lived. After the Battle of Midway a string of Japanese victories was followed by a long retreat. The yellow anchor badge on the field caps of these men show that they are naval troops and many garrisons on the Pacific Islands were manned by these troops.

Japanese naval landing troops look out over the barren terrain of the Aleutian Islands in June 1942. The two western islands of the Aleutians, Kiska and Attu, were occupied by the Japanese as part of the plan to move eastwards across the Pacific. Kiska was only about 900 miles from Fort Randall, the military base on the Alaskan peninsula. Following the defeat of the Imperial Navy at Midway in the same month the garrisons of the two islands were isolated and both were captured by US troops in August 1943.

This Italian cartoon from mid-1942 shows the victorious Japan clutching his new conquests with both hands. The supposedly comic caption says, 'Delicacies of the season – yellow sweetbreads'. Perhaps the irony of this cartoon is the difficulty that the Japanese Empire would now have 'holding on to' all the lands it had conquered. Although Japan's victory was an astounding achievement, governing such a far flung empire whilst at war was to prove to be an impossible task.